Teacher and Child Rights

TEACHER AND CHILD RIGHTS

Mrunalini Talla

SHIPRA

Rs. 900; US$ 36

ISBN: 978-93-88691-14-7

First Published in India in 2019

Teacher and Child Rights

Published by:
SHIPRA PUBLICATIONS
LG 18-19, Pankaj Central Market
I.P. Ext., Patparganj, Delhi 110092, India
Tel.: +91 11 2223 5152/6152, 9650028065
E-mail: info@shiprapublication.com
www.shiprapublication.com

Preface

The study is basically conducted with a serious concern for the children in schools. The way a teacher is dealing with children and how they treat a child inhumanly and victimise them differently. These issues are presented by focusing on the existing literature on child rights and also study-based results are presented. The study could explicate the perceptions of teachers and children and also personal observations. Some of the unique case profiles are also presented briefly anonymously. A module is planned and tried out on teachers to develop sensitivity to child rights.

This book would definitely be of use for any general reader interested to know about the child rights and protect them and academicians, scholars working in this area. It should help as reference for the students of teacher education and teachers interested in this area and are like a human teacher.

I put on record my sincere acknowledgements to UGC for its financial support without which it would have not seen the light. Never to forget the cooperation of the teachers, students, field assistants and project fellow and all other technical support from the department and UGC office at Osmania University, Hyderabad. I would express my gratitude to all those involved and also specially the publisher's initiative to create a space in their list and keep available for readers.

I put on record my sincere appreciation and regard for all the authors whose literature helped me in shaping this work. I acknowledge each one of them. I shall be obliged to all the intellectuals and readers making suggestions for improvement in future editions.

Contents

Preface 5

List of Tables 9

1. Introduction 11

2. Insights on Child Rights 30

3. Design of the Study 47

4. Teachers Awareness on Child Rights: Classroom Practices 55

5. Children Perceptions on School Practices and Functioning 62

6. Existing Status, Facilities and Teacher Practices 71

7. How Far Schools are Child Friendly? 82

8. Module on Child Rights for Training Teachers: Create Awareness on CRC 99

9. Reflections, Concerns and Future 111

References 121

Appendices 124

Annexures 138

Index 151

List of Tables

3.1: Sample Details 49
3.2: Sample Collected from the Field 49

4.1: Teachers Awareness on CRC 56
4.2: District wise Teachers Awareness on CRC in Percentage 57
4.3: Teachers Awareness on CRC 57
4.4: Teachers Awareness on CRC vs. Qualification in Percentage 58
4.5: Teachers Awareness on CRC vs. Gender in Percentage 58
4.6: Teachers Awareness on CRC vs. School Type in Percentage 59
4.7: Practices of Teachers in their Classrooms in Percentage 60
4.8: Facilities in the School in Percentage 61

5.1: Children's Perception on School 63
5.2: Children's Perception about their Teachers 63

6.1: Physical Dimension 71
6.2: Psychological and Emotional Dimension 72
6.3: Sexual Dimension 73
6.4: Restriction on Girls: Cultural and Social Dimensions 74
6.5: Teachers Concern about Children Health 75
6.6: Hygiene Practices in the School 76
6.7: Sanitary Facilities in Schools 77
6.8: Nutrition and Healthy Practices in the School 77
6.9: Type of School vs. Child Friendly Practices 78
6.10: School Facilities with Respect to Locality vs. Child Friendly Practices 78
6.11: Teachers Qualification vs. Child Friendly Practices 79
6.12: Teaching Subject vs. Child Friendly Practices 79
6.13: Teacher Age vs. Child Friendly Practices 80
6.14: Teaching Experience vs. Child Friendly Practices 80
6.15: Gender vs. Child Friendly Practices 80

7.1: School Facilities in Five Districts of Andhra Pradesh 82
7.2: Type of School vs. School Building 84
7.3: Locality vs. School Building 85

7.4: District-wise Space in the School Building 85
7.5: District-wise Aeration in School Building 86
7.6: District-wise Ventilation 86
7.7: School Type vs. Ventilation 87
7.8: Locality vs. Ventilation 87
7.9: District Wise vs. Space in the Classroom 88
7.10: School Type vs. Space in the Classroom 88
7.11: Locality vs. Space in the Classroom 88
7.12: District-wise School Ambience 88
7.13: District-wise Playground 89
7.14: Children allowed to Play in the School 90
7.15: School Type vs. Children are Allowed to Play 90
7.16: District-wise Adequate Furniture 90
7.17: School Type vs. Adequate Furniture 90
7.18: District-wise Separate Toilets for Girls and Boys 91
7.19: School Type vs. Separate Toilets for Girls and Boys 91
7.20: Locality vs. Separate Toilets for Girls and Boys 91
7.21: District-wise Availability of Scavenger 92
7.22: District-wise Drinking Water 92
7.23: District-wise Health Camps 93
7.24: District-wise Children with Neat Uniforms 93
7.25: District-wise Laboratory with Equipment/Chemicals 93
7.26: District-wise Teaching Learning Material (TLM) Available 94
7.27: Based on the Classroom Observations of the Teacher Practices 95
7.28: District-wise Child-Friendly Schools 95
7.29: Child to Child Interaction 96
7.30: Child to Teacher Interaction 96
7.31: Child to Teaching Learning Material 97
7.32: District-wise Disciplinary Practices 97
7.33: District-wise Child-Friendly Schools 98

8.1: Pre-and Post-test Results 102

Chapter 1
Introduction

Are children with or without rights?
A captivating ground reality

Though many rights are extended to children, do children really get the rights which are for them? In spite of RTE Act (2009) and its enactment from 01 April 2010, all that is expected is not much at sight.

A Captivating Ground Reality! Glimpse on a Child (Hema)

A 12-year-old girl child (Hema) is still in class IV along with other children who are around 8-9 years old. She is fourth girl child in the order of the family with five girls and a boy. In spite of RTE act, child is not in the appropriate class, age wise. The child is conscious of the fact and took her mother to the school to request the teacher to promote her to the higher class. But the teacher did not listen and continued the child in class IV and said it is difficult for the child to cope with higher class studies. The child experiences much humiliation to sit in the lower class with children much younger to her. Child says had my parents admitted me at the right time, I would have been in place along with my age group children. The child's expression about the family affairs and accepting the practices shows the helplessness of the child.

We are five sisters, two of my sisters got married. Seventeen years old sister (got married at the age of 14 years); 14 years old (got married at 13 years of age and now she gave birth to a male child). Since we are five girls, our parents try to get relieved by getting us married.

We (I and my sister) work as domestic servant and also go to government school. My parents say anyhow one day we will get married and go to other home but the future of the family, the torch bearer is my younger brother so he is sent to an English medium

> school, he joined at nursery level and is also sent for tuitions. The younger girl child of seven years old is yet to go to school. The child compromise and say it is a socially acceptable fact.

It is very obvious from the narrative that still there is gender discrimination in such families by the parents, neglect of the girl child to assist mother in household chores, sibling care and taking responsibility of home when parents are away to their village. The child also looks after the plastic containers (plastic vessels) kept outside their hut. They are physically exploited as they have to share the economic burden of the family also. Parents feel helpless about the whole scenario and they never feel that they are doing injustice to their children.

We see in one family child labour/domestic labour, age inappropriate class of study, child marriage, gender discrimination, out of school child. In many ways the rights of children are violated by their own parents. What would be our children's fate in future to come?

Such stories of girl children like Hema are plenty to record and narrate in almost every government school. Is it the negligence of the parents?, Poverty? Negligent attitude of parents towards the girl child?, Lack of awareness? Insensitive to child rights or basic human concern? Is it not far to reach the rights to many millions of children?

Conceptual Framework

How do we understand rights of the children?
What is the Convention on Rights of the Children (CRC)?
What does the history say about children's protection?
What is the role played by various agencies in this direction?
What are the measures taken by the Government of India?
What are the ground realities reflected in media about the children?

Responses to the above questions reveal clear insights into children's rights and their protection.

How do We Understand Rights of the Children?

The UN Convention on the rights of the child marked a turning point, recognising worldwide that children are not only subjects of protection but also holders of civil and political rights.

Mand de beur-buquiccho,
Deputy Secretary General, Council of Europe.

'CRC has set universal standards for the protection of children against neglect, abuse and exploitation as well as guaranteeing to them their basic human rights, including survival and full participation in social, cultural, educational and other endeavours necessary for their individual growth and well being'.

The child rights convention says that children have the right to be protected from physical, mental violence, degrading punishment, injury, neglect and abuse. They have the right to be protected from works that place them in danger, from drug abuse, sexual violence, trafficking and other forms of exploitation. They have the right to health, education, medical care and a decent standard of living. They also have the right to express their opinions, form organisations and participate in them.

UNICEF's mission is to advocate the protection of children's rights, to help meet basic needs and to expand their opportunities to reach their full potential. Children too have rights as human beings and also need special care and protection.

> "We cannot waste our precious children.
> Not another one not another day.
> It is long past time for us to act on their behalf."
>
> *Nelson Mandela and Graca Machel*

> "In you the future lives and thrives,"
>
> *Jawaharlal Nehru in a letter to children*

The basic premise of the convention is that the "Children are born with fundamental freedom and the inherent rights of all human beings". The largest gathering of world leaders in history assembled at the United Nations to attend the world summit for children on 29th and 30th September, 1990 led by seven heads of States and Government and 88 other senior officials at the Survival, Protection, Development of children and a plan of action for implementing the declaration in the 1990's.

The Convention on the Rights of the Child is the first legally binding international instrument to incorporate the full range of human rights—civil, cultural, economic, political and social rights. In 1989, world leaders decided that children needed a special convention just for them because people under 18 years old often need special care and protection that adults do not. The leaders also wanted to make sure that the world recognised that children have human rights too.

By agreeing to undertake the obligations of the Convention (by ratifying or acceding to it), national governments have committed themselves for protecting and ensuring children's rights and they have agreed to hold themselves accountable for this commitment before the international community. States parties to the Convention are obliged to develop and undertake all actions and policies in the light of the best interests of the child. (UNICEF: 2011).

Convention on the Rights of the Child (CRC) at a Glance

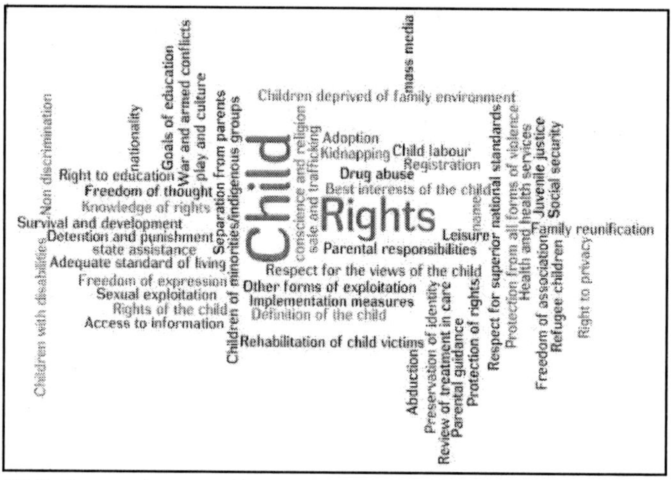

Fig 1.0: CRC Convention at a Glance

The convention is presented in three parts Part I, Part II and Part III

Part I (Articles 1–41)

Part I (Articles 1–41) includes various rights in the connection which can be categorised into four categories: Survival, Development, Participation and Protection.

The four basic principles (like four pillars) are reflected clearly in the following Articles:

1. Article 2: Non-discrimination
2. Article 3: Best interest of the child
3. Article 6: Right to life, survival and development
4. Article 12: Right to participate

Non-discrimination (Article 2) right to protect children from any form of discrimination.

All rights apply to all children without exception.

The child's best interest (Article 3)-the determining factor in all actions dealing with any child should be his or her best interest. In all cases, the best interests of the child take precedence over the interests of the adults concerned (e.g. parents, teachers and guardians). However, the question of how to decide on the best interests of the child remains difficult to determine and open to discussion.

> **Article 3.1** of the United Nations Conventions on the Rights of the Child (UNCRC) states that in all actions concerning children, whether undertaken by public or social welfare institution, courts of law, administrative authorities or legislative bodies, the best interests of the child shall be a primary consideration.

The rights to life, survival and development (Article 6) the right of the child to life is inherent, and it is the state's obligation to ensure the child's survival and development. This means that children cannot be subjected to the death sentence or to termination of life.

Respect for the views of the child (Article 12) the child has the right to express an opinion and to have that opinion taken into account in any matter affecting him or her. The Children's Convention is a powerful instrument, which by its very nature engages young people in an examination of their own rights. It is also an effective tool to assist people of all ages in identifying the complex responsibilities that go with ensuring these rights for children. Using the convention in this way will teach children how to advocate on their own behalf.

> **Article 12.1** Convention asserts that, states parties shall assure to the child who is capable of forming his or her own views the right to express those views freely in all matters affecting the child, the views of the child being given due weight in accordance with the age and maturity of the child' (UN 1989).

Part II (Articles 42–45)

Monitoring the Convention on the Rights of the Child

Like all human rights treaties, the Convention on the Rights of the Child contains articles that establish how governments' compliance with the treaty will be monitored.

Part II, Articles 42–45, of the Convention sets up these procedures and requirements:

a. It requires that governments make the rights in the Convention widely known to both adults and children (Article 42);

b. It establishes the Committee on the Rights of the Child, a body of independent experts that monitors implementation of the Convention on the Rights of the Child by its State parties (Article 43);
c. It requires states to report every five years on their efforts to implement the Convention (Article 44).
d. It encourages international cooperation in the implementation of the Convention, especially with specialised UN agencies such as UNICEF (Article 45).
e. These mandatory reports, usually prepared by a government agency specialising in children's issues, indicate who is not enjoying which rights, identify the constraints and obstacles to realising the rights and what the government intends to do to overcome these challenges. The report is presented to the Committee on the Rights of the Child in Geneva, where the Office of the United Nations' High Commissioner for Human Rights is based, which reviews it and makes recommendations for future action.

Part III (Articles 43-54)

Implementation Measures

These articles discuss how governments and international organizations like UNICEF should work to ensure children are protected in their rights.

Article 46: The present Convention shall be open for signature by all States.

Article 47: The present Convention is subject to ratification. Instruments of ratification shall be deposited with the Secretary-General of the United Nations.

Article 48: The present Convention shall remain open for accession by any State. The instruments of accession shall be deposited with the Secretary-General of the United Nations.

Article 49:

1. The present Convention shall enter into force on the thirtieth day following the date of deposit with the Secretary-General of the United Nations of the twentieth instrument of ratification or accession.
2. For each State ratifying or acceding to the Convention after the deposit of the twentieth instrument of ratification or accession, the Convention shall enter into force on the thirtieth day after the deposit by such State of its instrument of ratification or accession.

Article 50:

1. Any State Party may propose an amendment and file it with the Secretary-General of the United Nations. The Secretary-General shall thereupon communicate the proposed amendment to States Parties, with a request that they indicate whether they favour a conference of States Parties for the purpose of considering and voting upon the proposals. In the event that, within four months from the date of such communication, at least one third of the States Parties favour such a conference, the Secretary-General shall convene the conference under the auspices of the United Nations. Any amendment adopted by a majority of States Parties present and voting at the conference shall be submitted to the General Assembly for approval.
2. An amendment adopted in accordance with paragraph 1 of the present article shall enter into force when it has been approved by the General Assembly of the United Nations and accepted by a two-thirds majority of States Parties.
3. When an amendment enters into force, it shall be binding on those States Parties which have accepted it, other States Parties still being bound by the provisions of the present Convention and any earlier amendments which they have accepted.

Article 51:

1. The Secretary-General of the United Nations shall receive and circulate to all States the text of reservations made by States at the time of ratification or accession.
2. A reservation incompatible with the object and purpose of the present Convention shall not be permitted.
3. Reservations may be withdrawn at any time by notification to that effect addressed to the Secretary-General of the United Nations, who shall then inform all States. Such notification shall take effect on the date on which it is received by the Secretary-General

Article 52: A State Party may denounce the present Convention by written notification to the Secretary-General of the United Nations. Denunciation becomes effective one year after the date of receipt of the notification by the Secretary-General.

Article 53: The Secretary-General of the United Nations is designated as the depositary of the present Convention.

Article 54: The original of the present Convention, of which the Arabic,

Chinese, English, French, Russian and Spanish texts are equally authentic, shall be deposited with the Secretary-General of the United Nations. In witness thereof the undersigned plenipotentiaries, being duly authorized thereto by their respective Governments, have signed the present Convention.

The convention protects children's rights by setting standards in health care, education and legal, civil and social services.

The Convention on the Rights is unique. One of the main doctrines of the Conventions is that the 'child' is not alone; it considers the basic role of the parents and family for the welfare, care and protection of the children, also the need for the special protection of children who are separated or without families.

It considers the role of the community and state when required and the crucial contribution that can be made by international organisations and international cooperation. Moreover, the Convention provides a framework within. The child can make the difficult transition from infancy to adulthood.

CRC acknowledge the importance of family to a child's well-being and also recognises children as right-bearing individuals. It guarantees them as appropriate to their evolving capacity, the right to identity, to privacy, to information, to thought, conscience, and religion, to expression and to association.

The Convention has had enormous worldwide impact. It has intensified the child-rights efforts of UN agencies such as UNICEF and the International Labour Organization (ILO). It has affected subsequent child-rights treaties (e.g. Hague Convention on Inter country Adoption, which speaks of a child's right to a family rather than a family's right, to a child, and the Convention on the Rights of Persons with Disabilities). It has focused on international movements to stamp out pervasive forms of child abuse such as child prostitution and child soldiers, both of which are now the subjects of optional protocols.

Monitoring Children's Rights by UN and Non-Governmental Organisations

The UN often appoints an expert to serve as a Special Rapporteur to gather information on a critical issue or country. In response to international concern about the growing commercial sexual exploitation and the sale of children, in 1990 the UN General Assembly created the mandate for a rapporteur to gather information and report on the sale of children, child pornography and child prostitution.

A number of non-governmental organisations also monitor how the Children's Convention is being implemented. Some of these are large international children's advocacy organisations such as Save the Children and Child Rights Information Network (CRIN). Others operate at the regional and national levels. In Europe, for example, the European Network of Ombudsmen for Children (ENOC) investigates, criticises and publicises administrative actions that might be violating the CRC. The ombudsman can intervene separately from legal representatives, parents or guardians to represent the child's rights in a variety of civil or criminal cases where children are directly or indirectly involved. The Network includes representatives from Austria, Belgium, Denmark, Finland, France, Hungary, Iceland, Ireland, Lithuania, the former Yugoslav Republic of Macedonia, Norway, Portugal, the Russian Federation, Spain, Sweden and Wales. India has also set up a Commission for Children.

Promoting the Convention on the Rights of the Child

Civil society, children, teachers, parents and other agencies can play a major role in awareness raising and lobbying for action to promote child rights. To ensure that everyone who works with children as well as children themselves are aware of these rights, the Convention on the Rights of the Child should be available in school libraries and read and discussed in classrooms and with parents.

Theoretical Framework

There are two theoretical databases on child rights perspective:

1. The will or choice theory (Hart 1973; Summer 1987; Steiner 1994); the latter is the welfare or interest theory (MacCormick 1982; Raz 1984; Kramer 1998).

According to the will or choice theory a right is the protected exercise of choice. To have a right is to have the power to enforce or waive the duty of which the right is the correlative. This 'will theory' fits rights actively to do things (such as right to speak or to associate with others).

2. The welfare or interest theory finds a right as the protection of an interest of sufficient importance to impose on others certain duties whose discharge allows the right holders to enjoy the interest in question.

Children Rights: Outlook

(*See* Fig. 1.2)

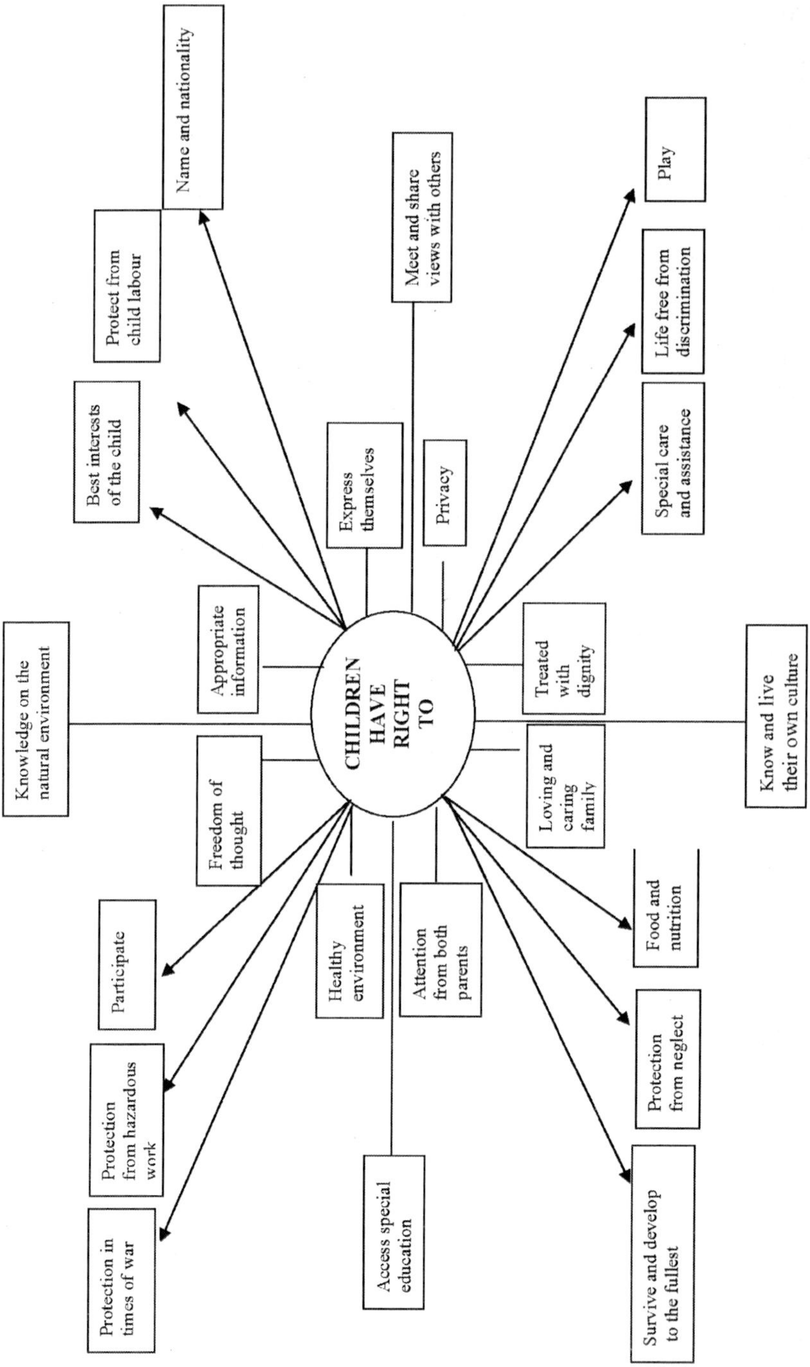
CHILDREN HAVE RIGHT TO
Name and nationality
Protect from child labour
Best interests of the child
Meet and share views with others
Express themselves
Privacy
Play
Life free from discrimination
Special care and assistance
Appropriate information
Knowledge on the natural environment
Treated with dignity
Know and live their own culture
Loving and caring family
Freedom of thought
Healthy environment
Attention from both parents
Participate
Food and nutrition
Protection from hazardous work
Protection from neglect
Protection in times of war
Access special education
Survive and develop to the fullest

Fig. 1.2

Status of Children

What are the facts before us about children which are very grave to note?

Every year, nearly 12 million children under the age of five die needlessly mainly from a handful of easily preventable childhood diseases. More than half of all South Asian children of this age are severely or moderately underweight, while nearly half of all under one's in sub-Saharan Africa is not immunised against common killer diseases.

Worldwide, 130 million children of primary school of which 1/3rd girls are not in the classroom, and thus denied the chance of a better future, while millions attend school where little learning actually takes place. One quarter of children in developing countries who start school cannot stay long enough to ensure lasting literacy. Nearly 250 million children are being robbed of their childhood because they are trapped in child labour.

Protection of Children Rights

Various organisations, committees and commissions brought to light many realities about children who accept and bear with and live in different circumstances.

What Efforts made in this Direction?

National Commission for Protection of Child Rights (NCPCR)

The National Commission for Protection of Child Rights (NCPCR) was set up in March 2007 under the Commission for Protection of Child Rights Act, 2005, an Act of Parliament (December, 2005). The Commission's Mandate is to ensure that all Laws, Policies, Programmes, and Administrative Mechanisms are in consonance with the Child Rights perspective as enshrined in the Constitution of India and also the UN Convention on the Rights of the Child (UNCRC). The Child is defined as a person in the 0 to 18 years age group.

The Commission visualises a rights-based perspective flowing into National Policies and Programmes, along with nuanced responses at the State, District and Block levels, taking care of specificities and strengths of each region. In order to touch every child, it seeks a deeper penetration to communities and households and expects that the ground experiences inform support field receives from all authorities at the higher level. Thus, the Commission sees an indispensable role for the State, sound institution-building processes, respect for decentralisation at the level of the local bodies at the community level and larger societal concern for children and their well-being.

Protection of Rights of Children by NCPCR

31. (1) The National Commission for Protection of Child Rights constituted under section 3, or, as the case may be, the State Commission for Protection of Child Rights constituted under section 17, of the Commissions for Protection of Child Rights Act, 2005, shall, in addition to the functions assigned to them under that Act, also perform the following functions, namely:

(a) examine and review the safeguards for rights provided by or under this Act and recommend measures for their effective implementation;
(b) inquire into complaints relating to child's right to free and compulsory education; and
(c) take necessary steps as provided under sections 15 and 24 of the said Commissions for Protection of Child Rights Act.

(2) The said Commissions shall, while inquiring into any matters relating to child's right to free and compulsory education under clause (c) of sub-section (1), have the same powers as assigned to them respectively under sections 14 and 24 of the said Commissions for Protection of Child Rights Act.

(3) Where the State Commission for Protection of Child Rights has not been constituted in a State, the appropriate Government may, for the purpose of performing the functions specified in clauses (a) to (c) of sub-section (1), constitute such authority, in such manner and subject to such terms and conditions, as may be prescribed.

32. (1) Not withstanding anything contained in section 31, any person having any grievance relating to the right of a child under this Act may make a written complaint to the local authority having jurisdiction.

(2) After receiving the complaint under sub-section (1), the local authority shall decide the matter within a period of three months after affording a reasonable opportunity of being heard to the parties concerned.

(3) Any person aggrieved by the decision of the local authority may prefer an appeal to the State Commission for Protection of Child Rights or the authority prescribed under sub-section (3) of section 31, as the case may be.

(4) The appeal preferred under sub-section (3) shall be decided by State Commission for Protection of Child Rights or the authority prescribed under sub-section(3) of section 31, as the case may be, as provided under clause (c) of sub-section (1) of section 31.

33. (1) The Central Government shall constitute, by notification, a National Advisory Council, consisting of such number of Members, not exceeding fifteen, as the Central Government may deem necessary, to be appointed from amongst persons having knowledge and practical experience in the field of elementary education and child development.

(2) The functions of the National Advisory Council shall be to advise the Central Government on implementation of the provisions of the Act in an effective manner.

(3) The allowances and other terms and conditions of the appointment of Members of the National Advisory Council shall be such as may be prescribed.

34. (1) The State Government shall constitute, by notification, a State Advisory Council consisting of such number of Members, not exceeding fifteen, as the State Government may deem necessary, to be appointed from amongst persons having knowledge and practical experience in the field of elementary education and child development.

(2) The functions of the State Advisory Council shall be to advise the State Government on implementation of the provisions of the Act in an effective manner.

(3) The allowances and other terms and conditions of appointment of Members of the State Advisory Council shall be such as may be prescribed.

Women and Child Development Government of India Planning Commission

Ministry of Women and Child Development, Government of India *Planning Commission Sub Group Report on Child Protection in the Eleventh Five Year Plan (2007-2012)* says that "among the millennium development goals child rights are embedded in Goal No. 3 Promote gender equality and empower women. It also says that in 2001 for the first time an attempt was made by Haq: Centre for Child Rights at using 'Child Budgeting' as a tool to monitor public funding on children through a decadal analysis of the union budget undertaken from a child rights perspective. Child budget analysis reveals the persisting low level of fund allocation for any measures affecting children, with resources for child protection at the lowest of all. The total share of child protection in the Union Budget for 2005-06 was just 0.034 per cent in financial year 2006-07 have remained more or less the same.

As regards protection of girl child rights is concerned, the working group of the Planning Commission says "an empowerment approach through *bala sanghas* (child associations) for them in schools in tandem with rights based approach needs to be adopted so that information and training inputs can be translated into decisions and behaviour changes. The aim needs to be to raise the profile of the girls and support them in becoming change agents for themselves, their peers and the community, in general". As regards communication strategy the working group says "deal with the girl child issue as though a strategy of adopting all measures to protect the girl child, and to secure her rights, must rest on the official position that she is heading towards becoming an endangered species. In this endeavour means of communication can play a key role. All channels and means of communication and dissemination need to be mobilised for Public Education to promote the equal rights and status of girl children, and to alert and inform the public against female foeticide, child marriage, discrimination and mistreatment, and all forms of gender injustice in childhood".

Child Rights Convention—Practised in Different Nations

The United Nations Convention on the Rights of the Child is a human rights treaty setting out the civil, political, economic, social, health and cultural rights of children. The Convention defines a child as any human being under the age of eighteen, unless an earlier age of majority is recognised by a country's law. (Article 1–CRC)

Nations that ratify this convention are bound to it by international law. Compliance is monitored by the UN Committee on the Rights of the Child, which is composed of members from countries around the world. Once a year, the Committee submits a report to the Third Committee of the United Nations General Assembly, which also hears a statement from the CRC Chair, and the Assembly adopts a Resolution on the Rights of the Child.

Governments of countries that have ratified the Convention are required to report to, and appear before, the United Nations Committee on the Rights of the Child periodically to be examined on their progress with regards to the advancement of the implementation of the Convention and the status of child rights in their country.

The UN General Assembly adopted the Convention and opened it for signature on 20 November 1989 (the 30th anniversary of its Declaration of the Rights of the Child). It came into force on 2 September 1990, after it was ratified by the required number of nations. Currently, 193 countries are party to it, including every member of the United Nations except Somalia, South Sudan and the United States. Somalia's cabinet ministers had announced plans in late 2009 to ratify the treaty.

Two optional protocols were adopted on 25 May 2000. The First Optional Protocol restricts the involvement of children in military conflicts, and the Second Optional Protocol prohibits the sale of children, child prostitution and child pornography. Both protocols have been ratified by more than 140 states.

States Party and Signatories

Australia is member of the convention since 1990. An article in the Australian National Observer in 1999 described it as having "frightening potential for the ultimate destruction of Western family values" and the Committee on the Rights of the Child as "an unelected body, which claims to be responsible only to the children of the world (and which therefore ultimately is responsible to no-one)".

Canada has ratified the Convention. Prior to ratifying the treaty, Canada's laws were in conformity with the treaty. Youth criminal laws in Canada underwent major changes resulting in the Youth Criminal Justice Act (YCJA) which came into effect on 1 April 2003. The Act specifically refers Canada's different commitments under the Convention.

The convention was influential in the following administrative Law decision of Baker v. Canada (Minister of Citizenship and Immigration).

Although the Islamic Republic of Iran is a state party to the Convention on the Rights of the Child, international human rights organisations and foreign governments routinely denounce executions of Iranian child offenders as a violation of the treaty.

The Republic of Ireland signed the Convention on the Rights of the Child on 21 October 1992 and ratified it. In response to criticisms expressed in the 1998 review by the UN Committee on the Rights of the Child in Geneva, the Irish government established the office of Ombudsman for Children and drew up a national children's strategy. In 2006, following concerns expressed by the committee that the wording of the Irish Constitution does not allow the State to intervene in cases of abuse other than in very exceptional cases, the Irish government undertook to amend the constitution to make a more explicit commitment to children's rights.

New Zealand ratified the Convention on 6 April 1993 with reservations concerning the right to distinguish between persons according to the nature of their authority to be in New Zealand, the need for legislative action on economic exploitation—which it argued was adequately protected by existing law, and the provisions for the separation of juvenile offenders from adult offenders.

Saudi Arabia ratified the Convention in 1996, with a reservation with respect to all such articles as are in conflict with the provisions of Islamic law and considers it to be a valid source of domestic law. The Committee on the Rights of the Child, which reviewed Saudi

Arabia's treatment of children under the Convention in January, 2005, strongly condemned the government for its practice of imposing the death penalty on juveniles, calling it "a serious violation of the fundamental rights".

The committee said it was "deeply alarmed" over the discretionary power judges hold to treat juveniles as adults: In its 2004 report the Saudi Arabia government had stated that it "never imposes capital punishment on persons. below the age of 18". The government delegation later acknowledged that a judge could impose the death penalty whenever he decided that the convicted person had reached his or her majority, regardless of the person's actual age at the time of the crime or at the time of the scheduled execution.

The United Kingdom ratified the Convention on 16 December 1991, with several declarations and reservations, and made its first report to the Committee on the Rights of the Child in January, 1995. Concerns raised by the Committee included the growth in child poverty and inequality, the extent of violence towards children, the use of custody for young offenders, the low age of criminal responsibility, and the lack of opportunities for children and young people to express views. The 2002 report of the Committee expressed similar concerns, including the welfare of children in custody, unequal treatment of asylum seekers, and the negative impact of poverty on children's rights. In September, 2008 the UK government decided to give up its reservations and agree to the Convention in these respects.

The United States government played an active role in the drafting of the Convention and signed it on 16 February 1995, but has not ratified it.

India has the distinction of having the largest child population in the world with more than one third of its population below the age of 18 years. The Constitution of India provided for the well being of children way back in 1950. The National Policy of Children formulated by the Government of India (GoI) in 1974 described children as 'supremely important asset'. The United Nations announced the Convention on the Rights of the Child in 1989, which was ratified by GoI in 1992.

What Efforts are Made in Indian Context?

In India, there is no outright ban on child labour, and the practice is generally permitted in most industries except those deemed "hazardous". Although a law in October 2006 banned child labour in hotels, restaurants, and as domestic servants, there continues to be high demand for children as hired help in the home. Current estimates as to the number of child labourers in the country range from the government's conservative estimate of 12 million children under 13 years of age to the much higher estimates of children's rights activists, which hovers around 60 million. Little is being done to address the problem since the economy is booming and the nuclear family is spreading, thereby increasing demand for child labourers. Under the auspices of the UNICEF financed UDISHA initiative the Government of India is specifying the outline of a means of change and improvement in child care.

There are severe restrictions on children in India on their rights to have a relationship with both parents, when they are separated/divorced, especially when laws to protect women and children (such as Domestic Violence Act, 2006 or Sec. 498A of Indian Penal Code) are abused or misused by women. The mother is provided custody by default with the child's access to the father not available or enforced in practice, even when there is a Court order to the effect. As a result, children's rights are often under-represented.

According to child labour in India statistics, child labourers in India consist of 50 per cent of the children in the country. In 2001 census statistics, there were about 12.7 million child labourers below fourteen years of age. This was an increase from the 11.3 million child labourers witnessed in the 1991 census. The census classified workers into main and marginal workers. When it comes to child labourers, those working as main workers, decreased to 2.3 per cent of the total population in 2001 from 4.3 per cent in 1991. However, the number of marginal child workers increased significantly so that the total number of children in the labour force increased. This indicates that most of the children are in hard casual labour where they work for long hours with meagre earnings.

The Department of Women and Child Development was set up in the Ministry of Human Resource Development in 1985. The Department, besides ICDS, implements several other programmes, undertakes advocacy and inter-sectoral monitoring catering to the needs of women and children.

What Efforts were made in this Direction to Protect Children?

In order to facilitate an open consultative process, a three day National Consultation Workshop was held in Delhi during December 1994 on CRC. India's first country report drawing extensively from these discussions was enriched with constructive suggestions given by the experts for full implementation of the Rights of the Child.

Subsequently, eleven state level workshops were held around the country at Jaipur, Calcutta, Lucknow, Hyderabad, Bangalore, Pune, Jabalpur, Patna, Ahmedabad, Bhubaneswar and Chandigarh in the course of 1994 to disseminate the provisions and to give an opportunity to the states to highlight their issues and make suggestions. There is a need to raise awareness and create an ethos of respecting the rights of the child in Indian society. We need to empower the younger generation to assert their basic rights in order to realise their full potential.

How is it Really Put on Record?

State governments to have a participatory process and give state's inputs for the CRC report. UNICEF will facilitate a participatory dialogue and children's participation will be welcomed in the states where it is present.

The nodal ministry, Ministry of Women and Child Development, will coordinate five regional consultations with NGOs and state governments to trigger the CRC process and invite feedback and inputs.

All central ministries dealing with children have been requested to provide analytical inputs on the progress and challenges in their sectors. Inputs are expected by the end of September from these various processes and the drafting of the report is expected to be completed by the end of December/January. The draft will then be shared with various ministries, state governments and cleared by the High-Level Committee before clearance by the Ministry of External Affairs.

Advocacy is ongoing for the discussion of the CRC Period report by the Parliamentary Forum on Children/Parliament prior to submission to the Committee on the Rights of the Child. (Jyothi Rao and Karuna Bishnoi).

What RTE Say About Child Rights?

The enactment of '*Right of Children to Free and Compulsory Education' Act* (RTE Act) in July 2009 is a step in the direction of guaranteeing right to education as a fundamental right. Through this Act, the State is obligated to ensure that no child is denied access to education in full-time formal schools, with standards and norms for schools clearly laid out. It is compulsory for the State to provide quality education at the earliest and to ensure that this education is imparted by trained teachers. This Act guarantees access to and retention in schools for millions of children across the country who are presently outside the school system, including child labour, street children, differently-abled children, orphans, and girls. It mandates that school drop-outs and out of school children are all mainstreamed and integrated to an age appropriate class.

Why is it Important to Go for a Study?

Many researchers prove that teachers, parents are not much aware of children's rights. Many teachers are not very keen and conscious of their practices in the classroom or in the school. Most of the school curriculum, teacher training and classroom practices are with teacher's dominant methods, subject centric curriculum and conventional mode of training. Teachers always feel that their role and decisions are more important. They feel children are weak, ignorant and needs support from the teachers. With these preconceived notion and established conventional approaches the system continues. Teachers create monotony and mechanical system in their regular teaching. They neither think as to how a child feels about their attitude, teaching, behaviour nor bother about or reflect themselves on children's issues. In spite of mandates for no corporal punishment in schools, child centric methods and curriculum, collaboration and participatory learning styles legally and otherwise. The conventional modes are still continuing. Huge funds are spent on various schemes to improve schools physically, qualitatively and academically. In view of the existing facts and ground realities, the present study intends to look into the various aspects related to schools to understand how far they are child friendly.

In view of the status of child rights existing in schools and the personal experiences with teachers working in schools and their disciplinary practices shows that there is a need to probe into the awareness levels of teachers and their sensitivity, practices in the classroom situations.

Keeping in view the study, funded by UGC for major research project, was conducted and same is being brought with the title 'Teacher and Child Rights' to create visibility to the rights of children and protection in schools.

Objectives of the Study

The following objectives have been framed for the study

1. To know the awareness levels of teachers on Child Rights.
2. To probe into sensitivity of teachers on issues related to Children.
3. To inquire into the practices of teachers in the classrooms.
4. To find out the perceptions of children on classroom practices.
5. To design a module on child rights for training teachers to create awareness among teachers.

Chapter 2
Insights on Child Rights

Independently not much effort is made by researchers in this direction. Mostly the insights are available from the Government, Non Governmental agencies at National and International level who are making a constant effort in this direction to bring into light many cases, issues related to children and making various interventions in the form of acts and advocacy.

The reviews scaffolded into the following heads and are compiled as:

1. Indian Constitution and other Acts
2. Human Rights Report (Quarterly)
3. UNICEF reports
4. National Commission for Protection of Child Rights (NCPCR) Reports
5. Save the Children
6. Other international lessons to learn
7. National learnings
8. What some Newspapers say

Before any of the intervention, acts and initiatives, Indian Constitution gave a clear promise to children along with adults. The Constitution of India offers all citizens, including children, certain basic Fundamental Rights—the right to life and liberty, the right to equality, right to freedom of speech and expression, right against exploitation, right to freedom of religion, right to conserve culture and the right to constitutional remedies for the enforcement of Fundamental Rights. Children are young citizens hence they enjoy these rights along with adults excepting those which they cannot exercise due to their being younger than the adults. Further, the Directive Principles of State Policy directs the State to ensure that all children are provided with services and opportunities to grow and develop in a safe and secure environment.

1. Indian Constitution Provision and Other Acts

The Constitution of India guarantees all children certain rights, which have been specially included for them. These include:

- Right to free and compulsory elementary education for all children in the 6–14 year age group (Article 45) as per RTE Act 21A, 2002 86th Amendment
- Right to survival (Article 21).
- Right to be protected from any hazardous employment till the age of 14 years (Article 24).
- Right to be protected from being abused and forced by economic necessity to entre occupations unsuited to their age or strength (Article 39(e)).
- Right to equal opportunities and facilities to develop in a healthy manner and in conditions of freedom and dignity and guaranteed protection of childhood and youth against exploitation and against moral and material abandonment. (Article 39 (f)).

Besides these they also have rights as equal citizens of India, just as any other adult male or female:

- Right to equality (Article 14).
- Right against discrimination (Article 15).
- Right to personal liberty and due process of law (Article 21).
- Right to being protected from being trafficked and forced into bonded labour (Article 23).
- Right of weaker sections of the people to be protected from social injustice and all forms of exploitation (Article 46).

2. Human Rights Reports (Quarterly)

Working Group on Human Rights in India and the UN (WGHR) 2011 in *Human Rights in India joint stakeholders' report United Nations universal periodic review* says that "India has 12 special laws for children apart from legal provisions in the penal and criminal codes. The *Juvenile Justice (Care and Protection) Act, 2000* based on a preventive approach to juvenile justice, poor implementation of the law, lack of support structures, low conviction rates and inadequate resources lead to derailment of justice. Children's courts were established by the *Protection of Child Rights Act, 2005*, Delhi was the first state to open such facilities for speedy trials in 2011. Protection of children still continues to receive only 1.26 per cent of the national budget".

Asian Centre for Human Rights in *India Human Rights Report Quarterly (January-June 2011)* says that, Child rights organisations claim that over 90 per cent of the children rescued by the department either ends up with the same employer or a different employer in less than a month's time. They claim that most children are not given counseling or even offered a place to stay after rescue. As per Child Rights and You (CRY), a total of 1,238 children had gone missing from eight districts of Delhi alone (the city has 11 police districts) during January–April, 2011, which means that over 10 children went missing from the capital every day. Around 468 (i.e. over 37%) remained untraceable. Delhi Police records stated that only 468 children went missing from 10 districts of Delhi between 1 January and 20 April, 2011. According to Amod Kanth of the Delhi Commission for Protection of Child Rights (DCPCR), in about 70-80 per cent cases, missing children are trafficked and used as labourers. As per Bachpan Bachao Andolan, more than 10,000 children in Delhi are living on the streets. Information received by BBA through the Right to Information Act revealed that during the period from 2006 to 2010, as many as 1,807 children escaped from the 26 recognised shelter homes due to poor conditions of the shelter homes. Out of these, 1,750 children (97%) remained untraced. At least 29 children died during the period 2006 to 2010. Surprisingly, 28 out of 29 children who died were from Bal Nirikshan Grih, Nirmal Chhaya Complex, Jail Road, Hyderabad.

Asian Centre for Human Rights in *India Human Rights Report Quarterly October-December 2010* says that "after inspecting 56 schools run by the BMC, the Mumbaiites for Child Rights (M4CR) found that most schemes, facilities and amenities entitled to a student of a BMC run school were confined only to paper. None of the 56 schools inspected had a first aid kit. The BMC pays an annual premium of rupees five crore to United India Insurance for the same but not a rupee had been given to students under this scheme".

Asian Centre for Human Rights in *India Human Rights Report Quarterly July-September 2010* says "on 1 August 2010, the National Commission for Protection of Child Rights (NCPCR) held a state-level public hearing on "Children's Right to Education and other issues" at Gandhi Bhavan in Bhopal. During the day long programme the panel heard 20 cases related to RTE and other issues. Some of the cases were: Diksha (14 years) and Priya (14 years) complained about regular and continuous sexual harassment at workplace (an under construction shopping mall) where they worked as child labourers. The girls wanted to study but could not do so as teachers push them out of school. Ganesh (11 years), a resident of Khera Kusalpur village in Neemuch district, cleared entrance test for admission in Navodaya Vidyalaya in Rampur on 10 September 2009 and was given admission on 23 June 2010. However, in the meantime he lost his eyesight in a mishap and on that ground his admission seemed to have been rejected. The jury members opined that Navodaya Vidyalaya violated norms and issued strict directives to the principal and Navodaya Sangathan to readmit the child. Rakesh Valmiki (12 years), a class V student of Government Primary School, Jaitpur, complained that he had to sit separately in school for being Scheduled Caste. He alleged that his teachers taunted that he belonged to the scavenger community, whose primary work is to clean toilets. Mamta Pathrod (16 years), a Dalit student was forced to leave school in 2009 because she was regularly beaten up and discriminated. Laxmi (13 years), a tribal student, of Harda district was not allowed to have mid-day meal with other students. The tribal students in the government school were even not allowed to touch drinking water pot. Laxmi also alleged that she was beaten up for touching cooked midday meal".

3. UNICEF Reports

UNICEF (2011) Annual Report shows, climate-related disasters, humanitarian emergencies, violent conflicts and economic turbulence all took their toll on children, especially the poorest. From the earthquake and tsunami in Japan to the severe flooding in Pakistan and the drought and famine in the Horn of Africa, UNICEF responded with our partners to alleviate the worst suffering, help communities rebuild and strengthen resilience for the future.

It significantly deepened implementation of equity agenda building on the principle that we must put first the rights of those children who are the most marginalised and most in need of our assistance. We do this not only because it is the right thing to do, but also because both research and experience show that it is the most practical and cost-effective thing to do, achieving greater results for children.

Nearly eight million children died in 2010 before reaching the age of five, largely due to pneumonia, diarrhea and birth complications. Some studies show that children living in informal urban settlements are particularly vulnerable. High urban child mortality rates tend to be seen in places where significant concentrations of extreme poverty combine with inadequate services, as in slums.

Around 2.5 million under-five deaths are averted annually by immunisation against diphtheria, pertussis and tetanus (DPT) and measles. Global vaccination coverage is improving: 130 countries have been able to administer all three primary doses of the DPT vaccine to 90 per cent of children younger than one. More needs to be done however. In 2010, over 19 million children did not get all three primary doses of DPT vaccination

UNICEF (2009), World Health Organization, the United Nations

Population Fund and the World Bank agreed to work together to help accelerate progress on maternal and newborn health in the 25 countries with the highest rates of mortality. Maternal deaths related to pregnancy and childbirth is an important cause of mortality for girls aged 15–19 worldwide, accounting for nearly 70,000 deaths each year. Early marriage and pregnancy, HIV and AIDS, sexual violence and other gender-related abuses also increase the risk that adolescent girls will drop out of school. This, in turn, entrenches the vicious cycle of gender discrimination, poverty and high rates of maternal and neonatal mortality. Educating girls and young women is one of the most powerful ways of breaking the poverty trap and creating a supportive environment for maternal and newborn health.

UNICEF (2009) focuses on maternal and neonatal health and identifies the interventions and actions that must be scaled up to save lives. Research indicates that around 80 per cent of maternal deaths are preventable if women have access to essential maternity and basic health-care services. A stronger focus on Africa and Asia is imperative to accelerate progress on maternal and newborn health. These two continents present the greatest challenges to the survival and health of women and newborns, accounting for an estimated 95 per cent of maternal deaths and around 90 per cent of neonatal deaths. Two thirds of all maternal deaths occur in just 10 countries.

UNICEF (2008) provided Ecuador with emergency education supplies and technical support, ensuring that 20,000 children remained in school despite severe floods, and helped more than 100,000 children in Haiti after hurricanes damaged or destroyed their schools. In war-torn Darfur, the Sudan, UNICEF provided learning material for more than 168,000 children, of whom 44 per cent were girls. And after a devastating cyclone, Myanmar received UNICEF assistance to reopen 2,300 schools and 343 early childhood development centres, allowing 315,000 children to continue their education with the minimum disruption.

UNICEF (2007), "Millions of children still not in school", reported that a right denied to millions of children worldwide. Some progress has been achieved over the past 15 years, with net enrolment for primary education in developing countries increasing from 79 per cent in 1990 to 86 per cent in 2004. "While we welcome the progress achieved over the last few years to send more boys and girls to school and help them acquire the basic skills they need to survive and thrive, it is unacceptable that millions of others still have no access to education," said Cream Wright, UNICEF also supports national policies that promote free and compulsory quality education in child-friendly schools that provide safe, healthy and gender-sensitive learning environments including health and nutrition services, and safe water and sanitation.

UNICEF (2007) "The State of the World's Children", observed that the need to eliminate gender discrimination and empower women and girls. The report argues that investment in women's rights will ultimately produce a double dividend, advancing the rights of both women and children.

UNICEF (2006), "The State of the World's Children 2007", UNICEF's flagship report argues that when women are empowered to make decisions, they are more able to fulfill their own rights and to support their children's rights as well.

UNICEF (2006), "The Millennium Development Goal on child mortality", observed that the Pneumonia causes almost 1 in 5 under-five deaths worldwide more than two million children each year. It kills more children than any other disease—more than AIDS, malaria and measles combined. Yet lack of attention to the disease means too few children have access to currently available interventions. This joint UNICEF/WHO publication is a call to action to raise awareness and reduce child mortality from pneumonia, which will contribute to achieving the Millennium Development Goal on child mortality.

UNICEF (2006) "1946-2006 Sixty Years for Children" Nations Children's Fund (UNICEF) 60th anniversary and traces, decade by decade, how the cause of children has evolved since World War II. This historical review explores UNICEF's contribution against a backdrop of rapid global changes in social, political and economic affairs—and looks ahead to 2015, the deadline for achieving the Millennium Development Goals that will transform the lives of millions of children.

UNICEF (2006) "The State of the World's Children 2007" examines the discrimination and disempowerment women face throughout their lives—and outlines what must be done to eliminate gender discrimination and empower women and girls. It looks at the status of women today, discusses how gender equality will move all the Millennium Development Goals (MDGs) forward, and shows how investment in women's rights will ultimately produce a double dividend advancing the rights of both women and children.

UNICEF (2004) "The State of the world's children" revealed that teachers should be trained sensitive to gender and child rights, and teachers should receive training in gender awareness in the classroom.

UNICEF (2004) "Increasing Awareness on CRC in Schools and Communities". The project strengthened the knowledge and increased awareness on Child Rights Convention (CRC) not only among children, but also among adults (teachers and parents).

UNICEF (2000) Annual Global publication "The lost children", examining the urban and rural education gaps, challenges facing orphans, lack of access to clean water, sexual exploitation, child soldiers and bounded labourers in factories and farms—all these and many more in India. A child between the age group of 0-14 years constitutes a little over one third India's population, constituting over three hundred million. Ironically they are the most vulnerable as they do not have any political constituency to represent their interest.

UNICEF (2000), "Children of the streets" study, showed that a correlation between economic hardship and arise in early marriage, even among some population groups that do not normally practice it.

UNICEF (1999), "Exclusive project for girl education" emphasised that the completion of quality primary education by all children, especially girls, in the age group of 6–14 years to enhance the learning outcomes of all children.

UNICEF (1999), The state of world's children report reveal that 130 million children in the developing world are denied this right and almost two-thirds of them being girls—nearly one billion people, or a sixth of the world's population are illiterate—the majority of them being women. This is a violation of rights and loss of potential and productivity that the world can no longer tolerate.

4. National Commission for Protection of Child Rights (NCPCR) Reports—Infocus

National Commission for Protection of Child Rights in Infocus (September 2011) says "In the past couple of months teams from NCPCR visited Amarabad Mandal, Mahboobnagar district, Andhra Pradesh, Dhanora block, Gadchiroli district, Maharashtra, Bishnupur district, Manipur, and East Champaran and Sheohar districts of Bihar, all predominantly tribal districts, to address complaints of child right violations in these areas. These are among the lowest performing districts in literacy, health and nutrition of children in the country. Some of them are also areas of civil unrest with a strong presence of Maoists. In spite of sub plans for tribal areas, unfortunately most of the facilities have not reached the children leading to greater disparities, marginalisation and perpetuation of poverty and inequality. They found that there was an enormous demand for education even amongst the poorest of tribal families. Pilferage of food supplies meant for midday meals is not the only complaint received by the National Commission for Protection of Child Rights (NCPCR).

After getting numerous reports on denial of child rights, a public hearing was organised by the Commission in Hyderabad to look into the matter in the last week of July. The team comprising Commission Chairperson Shantha Sinha, retired Justice Subhashan Reddy, Former Chairperson, Andhra Pradesh State Human Rights Commission, social activist J B Raju and Commission Members Ms. Dipa Dixit and Dr. Yogesh Dube looked into 37 cases of child rights violation.

These included cases related to the increase in out of school children and dropouts, migration, trafficking and child labour and children in need of care and protection. Raju, a student of Pier Giorgio Frassati High School in Nemmikal, Nalgonda district, stated the management of this private school had detained about 70 children of Class III, including him, because they had failed in their examinations. A petition made by Raju's father stating his son had the right to be promoted to the next class, was rejected by the school management on grounds that it was their prerogative to decide whom to promote. It was also disclosed that this school conducted screening tests for children seeking admission to all classes and imposed a fine of Rs.100 for each day that a child was absent from class. Another case that came up in the hearing was of Hemanth Sai, a student of Class III of Little Tom Primary School in Musheerabad, Hyderabad district. The school management had detained him in Class III because he had not paid his fees. His teachers refused to let him sit for the exams. Furthermore, they told him that he was incompetent and would not be admitted to any other school. The teachers also advised him to drop out of school and join the labour force to support his family.

In the case of Mandal Parishad upper primary school in Neriniki village, Kurnool district, 293 children were cramped into three small rooms and taught by only three teachers. When it rained, the school was flooded and so no classes were held. It was also pointed out that the government had still not given textbooks or any other entitlements due to the children of this school. Even the mandatory school management committee (SMC) had not been constituted to look into the matters of RTE implementation in the school. Many of the children of this school wishing to continue studies beyond Class IV had dropped out because of the lack of transportation between their village and the high school in Holagonda, 15 kms away. After hearing all the complaints, the Commission has written to S V Prasad, Chief Secretary, Andhra Pradesh, to ensure rights of every child in Andhra Pradesh were protected. It has given separate recommendations for each of the 37 cases. Copies of this letter have also been sent to relevant officials in the state and RTE State Representatives for action.

National Commission for Protection of Child Rights (NCPCR) on 19 May 2011 expressed displeasure over the functioning of the government agencies involved and asked the state government to immediately rehabilitate a child labourer who was rescued four months ago but not rehabilitated. The 8-year-old child was allegedly kept as bonded labourer and tortured by his employers. Nearly 550 school and college going girls reportedly went missing in Mysore district in 2010. The suicide of Rouwanjit Rawla, a student of premiere La Martiniere for Boys School, Kolkata, West Bengal raised national attention to the menace of corporal punishment. The school authorities rejected the recommendations of the National Commission for Protection of Child Rights to withhold two increments to the accused teachers. On 4 October 2010, the police arrested the principal and four other teachers for voluntarily causing hurt.

National Commission for Protection of Child Rights in *Infocus* September, 2010, the DCPCR served notices to the Organising Committee of the Commonwealth Games and various government agencies for alleged violation of the rights of the children of migrant labourers who were working at the Commonwealth Games sites. The DCPCR acted on a report by the NGO, Child Relief and You (CRY) which highlighted among others the lack of proper housing, quality food, sanitation, water, health care and education facilities for these children. The DCPCR asked various government authorities to examine the report and take appropriate action, including rescue, rehabilitation, and education of the affected children.

National Commission for Protection of Child Rights in *Infocus,* August, 2010 says that there is diversity among children and their privations are not all alike. A child who is orphaned, or whose family is displaced has different needs from one who is malnourished, differently abled, or subject to abuse and violence. One must recognise such particularities and offer services in order that children live with dignity and respect. In operationalising services for children it is essential to abide by the principle of non-discrimination and equality. A rights-based perspective regards all children as the same and provides them all with the same entitlements equitably. Those facing discrimination or those who are at a disadvantage, must be provided additional facilities through affirmative action to enable them to be at par with their peers. It also points out that an estimated 11 million street children live in India. Most of these children live in and around railway stations. In Delhi, Mumbai and Kolkata, street children, approximately 100,000–125,000 in each city, figure in the list of missing, runaway, abandoned or trafficked children. Lack of support puts them at risk from various forms of abuse and deprivation of rights that denies them a childhood.

National Commission for Protection of Child Rights, Shanta Sinha in Infocus, March, 2010 says that there is an urgent need to make all child related laws child centric not just child sensitive. The Indian Penal Code and the Criminal Procedure Code, which have subsisted since colonial times, are just not informed about child perspective and are definitely not child friendly or child centric. For example, the process of recording the statement of children who are victims is the same process that is used for adults and therefore, insensitive and often traumatic, resulting in further victimising the child. This becomes all the more important in the context of examining the need for a new law to address violence against children that includes sexual violence.

So there is an imminent need for all legislation related to children to focus on child jurisprudence and bring to the fore, a right based perspective in all Acts, criminal and penal procedures and in addressing violence and offences against children. The legal framework and the processes of rendering justice to children require constant review to be in sync with the rapidly changing society and must reflect the high ethical and normative standards of the time. The National Commission for Protection of Child Rights informed the Court those children from the north East Indian states were leaving their home states in search of education and were getting involved in trafficking.

National Commission on Protection of Child Rights Annual Report 2009-10 says that "the United Nations Convention on the Rights of the Child (UNCRC) elaborates the provisions of listening to the child, and the child exercising agency through child participation precisely because children are recognised as having the capacity to do so. This capacity is evolving and needs support and constant nurturing. Sometimes, when the children in question are very young, we as adults, and especially those in positions of trust either in the family or in institutions relating to children, must take responsibility for acting in a manner that ensures that children's interests are not compromised.

Dixit Dipa, Member, the National Commission for Protection of Child Rights at the National Convention on Displaced People (2008), in a seminar on *Universality of Child Rights—The Context of Displacement and Migration*, speaking about internally displaced children living in the camps says, "BECAUSE THEY ARE CHILDREN", irrespective of where they come from and where they have to go they have rights. Their entitlements and rights flow from the fact that they are citizens of this nation. The State and we as fellow human beings, have the obligation to fulfill the same".

National Commission for Protection of Child Rights in India (2008) report Abolition of Child Labour and Making Education a Reality for Every Child as a Right says that "there needs to be zero tolerance to children being out of school and being child labour achieved through free and compulsory education and abolition of child labour. The task of withdrawing a child from work therefore, becomes the same as inducting the child into school. The only form of school that does not explicitly support the concept of a child working is the formal day school. This automatically implies guaranteeing the right to education of all children in full time formal day school". It also points out that "it is important to appreciate the difficulties faced by the children of illiterate parents in schools and the lack of preparedness of the school system to absorb poor and first generation learner children".

National Commission for Protection of Child Rights in India—Sinha, Shanta (October 8–9, 2007) while addressing the Conference on the Rights of Children under six years towards Legal Framework organised by National Commission for Protection of Child Rights (NCPCR) in Vigyan Bhawan Annexe, New Delhi, on the child rights says "In the Indian context, the legal framework is an expression of the states' commitment to its precious citizens as well as of setting norms for society. It is only when the system begins to perceive violence and inequity in access to health, nutrition, education, and protection and is compelled to bring about substantial change in favour of children's rights that democracy is nurtured.

National Commission for Protection of Child Rights in India—Sinha, Santa (2007) in her "Children's Right to Education and Democratisation of Schools" says "schools are not equipped to appreciate the difficulties of the first generation learners. As a consequence, children are subject to insults and corporal punishments for not doing their homework, coming late to school, not wearing a school uniform, nonpayment of school fees and other school charges and so on. Children and their illiterate parents also find it difficult to cope with the myriads of procedures, rules and regulations that govern the school system and are therefore pushed out of schools, for reasons such as being unable to procure a medical certificate after a long absence due to illness. "There is an emergence of a large variety of private schools to respond to parental demand for education.

This has resulted in a differentiated school system reflecting class imbalances. Thus, on the one hand there are the inefficient and wasteful government schools struggling for resources and its students continuing to attend them in full faith that it is only education that can redeem them from the world of deprivation and vulnerability. Their survival in the school system under these circumstances is not by design but a sheer accident. Amidst the huge presence of government schools, there are on the other hand, fee charging one-room English medium private schools with untrained school teachers at one end of the spectrum and fully furnished air conditioned corporate schools at the other end. Private schools guided by the logic of the market have begun to sell their wares 'to each according to their ability'. Thus, there are as many schools as layers in the society.

Although the number of private schools and the children attending them are still small in number (estimated at about 20%) there is a trend in more and more numbers of children leaving government schools for the private schools. Such a mushrooming of private schools has a profound impact on the society as it reproduces class inequalities, fractures society into multiple layers, freezes mobility of its citizens to move up causing divisiveness and disharmony. This is contrary to the function that schools have always performed i.e. to bring together children across class, region, occupation, caste and other differences, to endow them with collective experiences and memories that enable

socialisation in a manner that allows the poor child to be on par with her peers, seizing opportunities with confidence. Schools have always been institutions for harmonising societies and enabling bridging the gaps among its citizens and fostering equality".

"Encouraging private schools as commercial enterprises compromises the principle of universality as it offers services only to those who can pay for it. Thus, those who are deprived and marginalised are automatically out of its net. If left unregulated, the higher end suppliers would foster further exclusion, and thus reinforce class differentiation. The rich and the poor would never meet and there is every possibility of widening the gap. It would operate inadvertently as a system of hidden apartheid. This is contrary to the very tenor of schools that have always been institutions based on universalistic principles, nurturing equity and social justice and fostering inclusive democracy". "It becomes imperative to see the role of schools as institutions that are indispensable for creating conditions for an inclusive democracy and as instruments for building capacities of the citizens".

The essential principle that guides State schools is that of inclusion as it cannot deny any child her right to participate in the school on any grounds. When it falters and creates structures and processes in a manner that children are excluded, the solution would be in reforming its system, rethinking its policies on education, making greater investments, embedded in a legal and normative framework as enshrined in the Constitution of India and taking forward the mission of schools for an inclusive democracy. Consequently schools become instrumental in democratising distribution of all those resources [technical and social skills, certificates, general capacities] enabling improvement of life chances and opportunities".

Education is seen as a great leveling process and a prerequisite for creating 'citizens'. Education being a public good must nurture and enhance the principles of inclusion, nondiscrimination, equity and justice.

5. Save the Children

Save the Children (September 2012). India's spending on health is abysmally low, a mere 1.67 per cent of the GDP in the 12th Plan. India is also likely to miss the Millennium Development Goal on child mortality. While under-five mortality declined from 107 in 1995 to 64 in 2009. At the present rate India will reach 54 against the target of 42 by 2015. Malnutrition is one of the biggest underlying causes of child mortality in India.

Save the Children (August 2010). Currently, 8.1 million children are out of school, seven million children are out-of-school in rural areas whereas 1.1million children remain out-of-school in urban areas. The survey shows eight out of ten among the middle class underestimate the levels of child mortality in India. Though nearly 60 per cent of those surveyed felt that the problem of child mortality was "very serious" in India, a shocking eight out of ten did not know that nearly two million children under the age of five die every year in India of diseases and conditions that are easily treatable and preventable. India has the highest number of children dying for any country in the world.

Save the Children (May 2010), Every year, close to two million children die before their fifth birthday and around 67,000 women die annually from complications related to pregnancy and childbirth. It is estimated that 74 per cent of mothers' lives could be saved if they had access to a skilled health worker at delivery and emergency obstetrics care for complications, and 63 per cent of children under five could also be saved if all children were to receive a full package of essential health care that includes skilled birth attendance, immunisations and treatments for pneumonia, diarrhea and malaria.

Save the Children (2006) says every 20 seconds, a child under-five dies in India. Close to 1.7 million children under the age of five die every year in India.

Save the Children (2006) West Bengal, Mohendernath Ray: Abuse among child domestic worker revealed that child abuse: physical, emotional and sexual is widely prevalent among the child domestic workers, irrespective of their gender, and is mostly perpetrated by their employers or family members of their employers. It has also been observed from the collected data that even when the abuser is not someone from the employer's family, it is someone associated with the family in some way or the other. In this way, the abuse (and abuser) has a strong link with the child's status as a domestic worker in that household.

6. Other International Lessons to Learn

International report of Australian Child Rights Task Force Report (2011)—"Listen to Children" developed after consultations with 750 children and 100 organisations along with the Australian Federal Government and Australian Human Rights Commission points out that "despite ratifying the United Nations Convention on the Rights of the Child in 1991, this report finds that Australia has not effectively incorporated human rights into policy and legislative frameworks to nurture and support children. Instead, successive governments have perpetuated a traditional welfare approach to children's wellbeing and have not learned to listen to and work with children to create child-sensitive bodies, systems and initiatives."

Central African Republic (CAR) May 2011—Children Face Recruitment Risk, May 2011—Peter 13, is afraid of going to sleep some nights because when he closes his eyes, he sees things he doesn't want to remember. "I see someone doing bad things to people and I think it's me," he says from his home in Central African Republic (CAR). A former child soldier snatched by rebel fighters from the Ugandan Lord's Resistance Army (LRA), Peter recalls the atrocities—looting, killings and abductions—he was forced to commit alongside other children. Hundreds of children like Peter are being kidnapped, recruited into armed groups and denied humanitarian help in CAR, the Watch list on Children and Armed Conflict (Watch list) and the Internal Displacement Monitoring Centre (IDMC).

Democratic Republic of the Congo DRC (May 2011) Congo's Children Vulnerable to Sexual Exploitation May 2011—Congo's women and children remain vulnerable to poverty, commercial sexual exploitation as well as sexual violence related to the country's long-standing conflict. Children living in the Democratic Republic of the Congo (DRC) are being exposed to life-threatening forms of neglect brought because of poverty. Congolese families can have as many as 10 to 12 children in the same household. This creates a family dynamic that changes the relationship between parents and their children. Parents 'primary concerns become the survival of the entire family, instead of the welfare of each individual child. The result of this is that children tend to bear the burden of parental stress and poverty.

Human Rights Watch Report (2003)—"Trafficking in children" observed that the trafficking of girls into domestic and market work and the trafficking of boys into agricultural work.

UKIERI funds research on Children's Rights in India and the UK Law, Policy and Outcomes. It is working towards increasing public discourse and awareness towards recognition of child rights and the obligation of states and societies to protect promote and fulfill their rights and enabling effective interaction with the state and civil society organisations on a firmer theoretical and practical foundation.

Azerbaijan (2002)—A Survey conducted and revealed a gender gap in learning achievements in terms of literacy, numeric and life skills among children leaving primary schools.

The Back to School Campaign in Afghanistan (2002) showed what is possible when the international community is seriously committed to tackling a crisis starved of education throughout the years of conflict but particularly under the Tailbone, the hunger of Afghan children for chance to go to school was over whelming.

The Bangladesh Shishu Adhikar Forum (2002)—Annual Report on "Child Rights in Asia" revealed that 7445 children were violated in 2002; 3776 children killed every day; 686 girls/women were raped; and 83 of them were killed after rape.

In Malaysia, 800 cases of child abuse were reported mostly related to physical and sexual abuse of girls. 3609 incidents related to the exploitation of children, sexual exploitation of children, trafficking, forced prostitution, child labour exploitation, child death, missing children and children in conflict with the law were recorded by the child workers in Nepal.

Child Protection Foundation (CPF) (2002) revealed that the 215 children were raped, 164 abused and UNICEF estimated that there were at least 2,00,000 child prostitutes in Thailand, in Pakistan 825 minor Boys, 614 minor girls. Nafeesa al-Jaefee (2002) "Importance of revamping the university curriculum", the secretary-general for the higher council of motherhood and childhood emphasised the importance of revamping the university curriculum through adding the issue of children's rights to the curriculum, especially to the faculty of education. "Teachers are the primary source of development in children. They interact directly with children so they have to be qualified enough to carry out their responsibilities."

The project SACP (February–December 2002), "Internet and Child Rights" with the support of the UNDP in Bulgaria, Protection from exploitation or involvement in illegal activity through Internet." Through this Project SACP (State Agency for Child Protection) offered specific answers to the necessity of a contemporary state policy directed to awareness rising on child safety in Internet and to effective protection of their rights as Internet users.

Evaluation report (2001)—"Rights and Equity in the Classroom" A Case Study of Classroom Interactions in Basic Schools in Ghana, revealed that no clear-cut policy documents on rights and equity issues exist though gender equity and child rights appear to be the objective of some interventions of the sector.

BALL (1999), "Awareness of teachers on child rights" found that pressure for performance results in teachers narrowing the classroom experience and focusing on students who testify to their teaching ability.

Informal Sector Service Centre (1998), "Child rights awareness training" observed that no concerted effort has been made to improve the ground situation of the children in Pakistan, and socio cultural attitudes make the exploitation of the child manifold. So, there is a need that the rights and responsibilities of the all stakeholders involved in rearing a child should be made clear for the establishment of the healthy boundaries of the child's personality and to save him from being a prey of abuse.

7. National Learnings

Gideon Promono (2005), "Acehnese teachers educated in child rights" emphasised that the, "Teachers are key players in society. Creating awareness about children's rights through teachers will provide better results."

Nalini Juneja (2005), "The Right of Children in School to be free from fear" emphasised that prohibition of corporal punishment in proposed Right to Education Bill. No child shall be awarded physical punishment in any form in a school.

Magu Madhura Kalike (2004), "Awareness of teachers on child rights" revealed that they saw the positive changes in teacher attitudes towards the children, many teachers who realised that they lack the proper education information have now come forward to be trained in the same.

Kapherine Covell (2004), "It's Time Children's Rights Education", revealed that when children learn about their rights they identify better with all others because they realise that they share the same rights. In the words of one grade eight teachers.

Action Research on Trafficking in Women and Children in India (2002–2003), has brought out some important facts and figures regarding trafficking. It has illustrated a strong linkage between trafficking and migration. It has provided us with the understanding, addressing the vulnerability of migrants is an important tool to prevent trafficking. There is an added dimension in trafficking because of unconventional means of commercial sexual exploitation like sex tourism and exploitation in massage parlors, beer bars, etc. These have created a high demand for children. There are not many initiatives to understand and address these issues except for a few like the Goa Children's Act, 2002. Similarly, a clear linkage has been established between trafficking and those reported missing. It has also brought to light that an average of 22,480 women and 44,476 children are reported missing in India every year. Out of which 5,452 women and 11,008 children continue to remain untraced.

8. What Newspapers Say

What are the Ground Realities Reflected about the Children in the Media?

How child rights are being violated in various walks of life? Those who are the protectors are themselves indulging in violating the rights in various contexts parents, teachers, police, own relations. It is very heartening and astonishing to read innumerable instances which are reported and notified in the media. There can be much more violations and many more instances which went unnoticed and unreported.

However, to mention a few news items and a few clips which are negative and a few positive drafted here (See annexure).

Other Newspaper Stories (*See* annexure, pp. 138-141)

What lessons are already made available for us to grapple the issues related to child?

- A school child studying Class X was given punishment by the teacher to stand throughout the day, died after a few days. Madannapet, private school….
- David Grimson son Alistair, who was killed by stray bullets in a gun fight, at the base of a mock tombstone which the control arms coalition set up next to the United Nations building in New York. Everyday 2000 people are killed by arms.
- Similarly, it is reported that three tribal children die in ashram school in Vizianagaram, Tampalapadu.
- Tutor tortured two children for not doing homework.
- Seven year old girl and four year old boy were beaten up by cell phone charging wire at Kothapet (*The Hindu* Newspaper).
- Man kills his three year old daughter for crying continuously at Medikunda village in Medak Mandal (21, July, *The Hindu* Newspaper).
- Two children die after eating chocolates at Devarakonda.
- Man tortures nine year old son for not doing well in studies by branding the boys back with a spatula at Ramayapet (*The Hindu* Newspaper).
- Father molested his own girl child of 13 year old.

Many more children are also deprived of their right to education being in varied disadvantageous circumstances, street children, runaway, rag pickers, etc.

- Some positive stories too exist like 12 children rescued from bonded labour.
- Girl child is set free from child marriage.

Chapter 3

Design of the Study

The procedures adopted for the study are discussed here.

Field Visit

The field survey was conducted in five districts of earstwhile Andhra Pradesh namely Hyderabad, Ranga Reddy, Mahabubnagar, Medak and Nalgonda districts before identification of the sample and designing of the tools. Very informal discussions were held with the teachers, students and the other education officers. It was observed at some places teachers were given training on child rights practices. They shared a training module but are not very clear in their know-how on the practices in protecting children's rights. With the insights from the field, the principal investigator planned the methodological procedures.

Hypotheses

1. There will be difference in the awareness level of teachers on child rights.
2. Teachers are not sensitive towards issues related to children.
3. Teachers show child-friendly practices in the classroom.
4. There will be difference in the perceptions of children on classroom practices
5. Module will develop awareness in teachers on children's rights.

Method

Both qualitative and quantitative methods of research were planned to utilise for the purpose of the study. By and large it is a survey to capture the opinions of the teachers and children. Also study involves observation by the field assistants and the investigator to get deep insights into the existing practices of teachers in schools with regard to child rights based issues.

Research Design

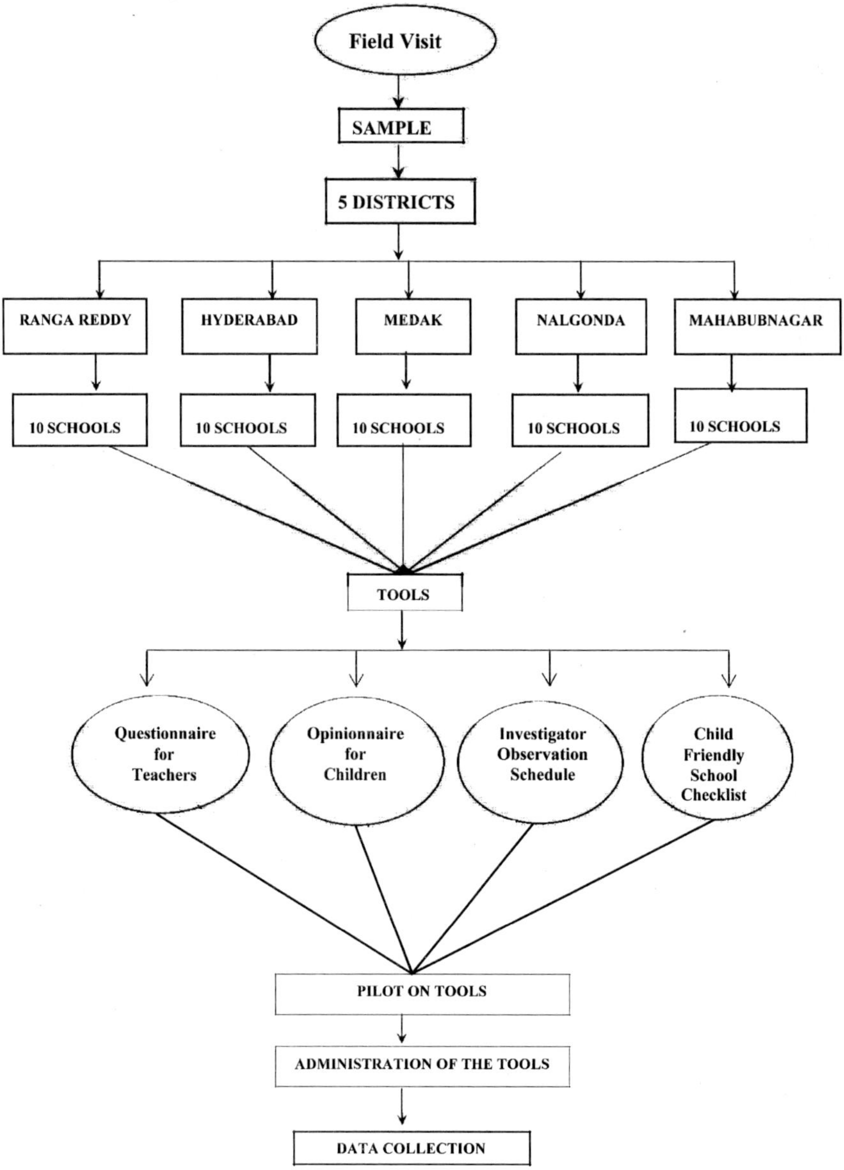

Fig. 3.1: Flowchart of Research Procedures

Sample Planned

What are the Details of Sample Planned?

Sample is planned to draw 500 teachers, 250 students from five districts of Andhra Pradesh as detailed below. 100 teachers and 50 students will be drawn from each district. Both male (50) and female (50) teachers from each district will be included in the sample. i.e. 250 female and 250 male teachers on the whole are included in the sample. From each districts 50 children (25 girls and 25 boys) will be included in the sample i.e. 125 boys and 125 girls from 10 schools in each district.

Table 3.1: Sample Details

Sl. No.	*Districts*	*No. of Schools*	*No. of Teachers*	*No. of Children*	*Total*
1.	Ranga Reddy	10	100	50	150
2.	Hyderabad	10	100	50	150
3.	Medak	10	100	50	150
4.	Nalgonda	10	100	50	150
5.	Mahabubnagar	10	100	50	150
	Total	**50**	**500**	**250**	**750**

What Actually Got from the Field?

Table 3.2: Sample Collected from the Field

Sl. No.	*Districts*	*No. of Schools*	*No. of Teachers*	*No. of Children*	*Total*
1.	Ranga Reddy	11	100	74	174
2.	Hyderabad	10	100	59	159
3.	Medak	15	100	114	214
4.	Nalgonda	13	99	69	168
5.	Mahabubnagar	13	100	76	176
	Total	**62**	**499**	**392**	**891**

Data Collection Tools

The following tools designed keeping in view the objectives framed for the study.

1. Questionnaire for teachers
2. Opinionnaire for children

3. Observation schedule for the investigator—classroom observation.
4. Child friendly school facilities checklist.

Development and Description of the Tools

Development and description of the tools are presented below:

Tool 1: Questionnaire for Teachers

Questionnaire is designed to get the information from teachers with regard to their awareness on child rights convention (CRC) and their practices in the classroom. The questionnaire consists of three parts. They are:

Part A: Profile of the teachers
Part B: Awareness on child rights convention
Part C: Practices of teachers in the classroom.

Part A includes personal details of the teachers like age, qualification, gender, religion, community, type of school and locality.

Part B includes items related to child rights convention (CRC). It includes 31 items related to the provisions made in the child rights convention like number of inclusions, categories of rights, rights related to protection, education, health, child participation, etc.

Part C includes 29 items. The items 1-25 are related to the practices of teachers in their classrooms such as the categories of children join their schools, encouraging children to come to school regularly, reasons for dropout, academic activities, giving awareness to parents and children about the benefits, methods of teaching, treatment of children, teaching learning strategies, materials, equipment and teaching aids and other practices of teachers.

Item 26 focuses on various facilities available in their schools like teaching-learning materials, physical facilities, classroom environment, sanitary and other academic facilities.

Item 27 and 28 covers the assessment at school and finally item 29 is an open ended question on best practices in their schools respectively.

Standardisation of the Tool

Both validity and reliability was established by trying out on 10 per cent of the sample other than the sample selected for the study. Item wise validation was done. Thus, the content and construct validity is established.

Reliability: Split half method was used to establish the reliability of tool. The co-efficient correlation between two halves (0.721) was found to be high. Thus, from the results obtained it can be stated that the tool possess reliability.

Scoring: For the correct answer one score and for the wrong answer zero score was given

Tool 2: Opinionnaire for Children

It is designed to know the opinion of children about their teachers, school facilities and functioning of their school.

Part A: Profile of the child
Part B: School facilities
Part C: Open ended questions about their teachers teaching in the classroom and narrative on the functioning of their school.

Part A include child details like age, class, gender, school, type of family, number of family members, occupation and qualification of parents, locality.

Part B includes school facilities: items from 1-7 related to the school environment and basic facilities; items 8-28 related to teachers care and concern towards the children, treating all children equally, teaching the lessons interestingly and motivating the child; item 29 is open ended question asking the students to give a narrative about their liked teacher.

Part C consists of 14 items of which 10 items are open ended questions, items 1-10 are related to teachers, teachers teaching in the class, students pleasant, unpleasant and other memorable experiences in the class/school. From 11-14 the students are asked to write a story on the functioning of their school and their views about how the school should be.

Standardisation of the Tool

Validity: Both validity and reliability was established by trying out on 10 per cent of the sample other than the sample selected for the study. Item wise validation was done. Thus, the content and construct validity is established.

Reliability: The tool was tried out with 10 per cent of the sample other than the selected sample for the study. Split half method was adopted to find out the reliability. There is a high positive correlation (0.762) was noted from the results. Thus, the tool possesses reliability.

Scoring: For the answer 'yes' one score and for 'no' zero score is assigned.

Tool 3: Investigator Observation Schedule (Classroom Observation)

It is designed to observe the sensitivity of teacher in the classroom and the way they treat the children. The item related to psychological and emotional, sexual, cultural and social context are included. The observation schedule ends with open ended questions to share any other information related to their school and students.

Part A: Profile of the teacher
Part B: Teacher treatment of the children in the school/classroom

Part A includes personal details of the teachers like, age, qualification, gender, religion, community, type of school and locality.

Part B consists of five dimensions. The first dimension includes items related to physical treatment of the children by the teacher, second dimension includes items related to psychological and emotional, third dimension includes items related to sexual harassment by the teachers, fourth dimension covers social and cultural restrictions, and fifth dimension is related to health, hygiene and nutrition of children.

Standardisation of the Tool

Validity: Validity was established by trying out on 10 per cent of the sample other than the sample selected for the study. Item wise validation was done. Thus, the content and construct validity is established.

Scoring: As per the observation schedule criteria, if parameter is present then one score is assigned and if it is not present zero score is assigned. Likewise each criteria is observed and the scores are assigned for all the observations.

Tool 4: Child Friendly School Facilities Checklist

It is designed to check the facilities available in the school. It includes school children particulars, teacher practices in curriculum transaction, child-child interaction, child-teacher interaction and child-teaching and learning material, discipline in classroom.

Part A: Physical facilities of the school, school children particulars
Part B: Classroom observation or informal talk with the teachers
Part C: Practices of teachers in classroom during curriculum transaction, child-child interaction, child-teacher interaction and child-teaching and learning material, discipline in classroom.

Part A is related to physical facilities. Items 1-24 include school building, aeration, ventilation, playground, furniture, availability of dust bins for safe disposal, toilet facilities for girls and boys, maintenance of classroom, availability of drinking water, conduct of health camps, mid-day meals. Items 25–40 consists of school children particulars like total strength of the school, total number of boys and girls, number of children from low socio-economic background, number of school drop-out children, Teaching Learning Material (TLM), laboratory equipments, recreation facilities.

Part B includes classroom observation or informal talk with teachers. Items 1-24 include teachers attitude towards children, appreciate the good looking children and neglecting the slow learners. Motivate, encourage boys and girls equally, being patient and tolerant with children, guides, directs them and attend to their health problems. Helping children in various contexts like learning difficulties, financial problems, family support and counseling.

Part C consists of practices of teachers in classroom curriculum transaction. Items 1-4 include teachers interaction with the students in the classroom, 5-19 include classroom environment for the students to learn, teaching the concepts clearly by taking the examples related to everyday living, giving freedom to express student's feelings and motivate the child to learn, respect the child's interest. Items 20-22 deal with child-child interaction, child-teacher interaction and child-teaching and learning material interaction. Items 23-32 focus on discipline of children and teachers efforts to make every child to speak and take part actively.

Standardisation of the Tool

Validity: Item wise validation was done. Thus, the content and construct validity is established.

Scoring: As per the item related to the practices observed one score is given and if not observed zero score is assigned.

Administration of the Tools and Collection of Data

As per the proposal, in order to collect the data on time and avoid delay in the project completion with the authorities' permission, 10 field assistants were identified and got approval. For each district two field assistants were appointed to collect the required data. Before sending assistants to their respective districts to collect the data uniformly all the field assistants were given orientation. Care was also taken while selecting the field assistants those who are already into M.Phil., Ph.D research work and are exposed to collection of data in order to avoid gaps.

From each district as per the sampling design the data were collected. Field assistants felt it was very difficult to get the responses from teachers. Teachers are scared to say that they have no idea on any specific child rights aspects and were very reluctant to respond. Further, most of the teachers did not show any interest in filling up the schedules. Some teachers did not cooperate to observe their classroom teaching which put the field assistants to difficulty in many schools. In some schools photo/video was not allowed as they felt that assistants are going into their privacy. However, the field assistants in some districts covered data more than the expected by discarding the incomplete and non-cooperating schools data.

However, after much difficulty by building rapport with the school teacher and children, required data were collected and same was cleaned and submitted to the principal investigator. The project fellow coordinated with the guidance of the principal investigator to collect the data objectively. While administering the tools, care was taken to take necessary permission from the schools and fixing up the schedules to visit the schools to sit and informally talk to the children and teachers. The collected data were organised systematically for data entry. The data were entrusted to the data entry operator to entre the data for further analysis.

Chapter 4
Teachers Awareness on Child Rights

Classroom Practices

How far the Teachers have Awareness on CRC?

To get an overall view on the level of awareness that teachers have on CRC, holistically their responses were sought and the insights are brought to light (*see* Table 4.1).

It is very discouraging to note that most of the teachers (79.2%) have very low awareness on child rights convention (CRC). More than half of the teachers (53.1%) never read the convention and (70.1%) have not undergone any training on CRC. Teachers (98%) could not even say when the UN General assembly adopted CRC. Also teachers (80.6%) could not say that on 11 December 1992 CRC was acceded by Indian Government. Hardly any teachers (4.4%) know 1 January 1979 as International year of the child. Teachers (80.2%) have no idea as to how many countries (193) ratified UNCRC. Almost 76.2% of teachers do not even know that 'children below 18 years of age' is considered as child according to CRC. Very few teachers (11.6%) have known about the inclusions (54 Articles) in CRC. Teachers (87.2%) really do not know that CRC is being presented in three parts. Only few teachers (7.6%) have awareness on the number of rights (41 Articles) which are included under Part I of CRC. Even teachers (4.4%) have no idea about the four inclusions in Part II and some teachers (4.2%) do not know Part III has nine inclusions. About a quarter (24.6%) teachers know that there are four categories of rights Survival, Development, Protection and Participation.

It is very sad to know that not even 1/5th of teachers know the important rights of children like the Article 2 right to non-discrimination (6%), Articles 3 protection and care (17.4%), Article 6 right to life, survival and development (18.8%), Article 12 right to express their views (17.8%).

Many teachers (86.4%) do not even know that Article 28 in CRC is related

Table 4.1: Teachers Awareness on CRC

Sl. No.	*Teachers Awareness on CRC*	*Yes Percentage*
1.	Did you read the child rights convention?	46.90%
2.	Did you get any training on child rights?	29.90%
3.	10 December 1948 UNGA adopted the UDHR	22.60%
4.	20 November 1989 UNGA adopted the CRC	10.20%
5.	11 December 1992 the GoI adopted the CRC	19.40%
6.	1 January 1979 is international year of the child	4.40%
7.	193 countries have ratified the CRC	19.80%
8.	USA and Somalia not ratified the CRC	4.60%
9.	Below 18 yrs is considered as a child	23.80%
10.	54 articles are there in the CRC charter	11.60%
11.	Three parts/divisions are there in CRC charter	12.80%
12.	41 articles are present in Part-I	7.60%
13.	Four articles are present in Part-II	4.40%
14.	Nine articles are present in Part-III	4.20%
15.	Four categories are there in CRC	24.60%
16.	Art 2 deal with non-discrimination	6.00%
17.	Art 3 deals with protection and care	17.40%
18.	Art 6 right to life, survival and development	18.80%
19.	Art 12 right to express their view	17.80%
20.	Art 28(a), Art 29 are pertaining to education	13.60%
21.	Art 19 focus on child abuse	5.60%
22.	Art 32 Protect from economic exploitation	21.40%
23.	Art 34 Protect from sexual exploitation and abuse	12.80%
24.	Art 23 gives provision to the disabled children	20.80%
25.	Art 2,40 represent Right to Participation	13.60%
26.	On what basis child is discriminated in class?	7.00%
27.	Art 28, 29 CRC is similar to Art 45 of IC	7.60%
28.	Art 19 is pertaining to violence	7.00%
29.	>18 age children are recruited to armed forces	15.20%
30.	Children >14 yrs are considered as child labours	23.20%
31.	Who should inform children about their rights?	38.30%

to education. Only few (5.6%) teachers are aware that Article 19 is pertaining to child abuse. About 1/5th (21.4%) teachers know that article 32 protects children from economic exploitation. A very few teachers (12.8%) know that Article 34 protects the children from sexual exploitation. However, some teachers (20.8%) know that Article 23 made the provision for disabled children. Only few teachers (13.6%) know that Articles 2, 40 represent children's right to participation. Only few teachers (7%) recognised that children are discriminated in the classroom. Similarly, very few (7.6%) teachers know that Article 45 of Indian Constitution is being represented in Article 28, 29 of CRC. Just a few (7%) teachers have the awareness that Article 19 is pertaining to violence. Most of the teachers (84.8%) do not know that children can be recruited to armed forces only after 18 years of age. The long time concern related to child labour is known to only some teachers (23.2%) children who are below 14 years of age if engaged in work they are considered as child

labourers and their rights are protected through CRC. Mostly teachers (61.3%) are unaware that it is their responsibility along with parents to inform children about their rights.

The results reveal a poor level of awareness among teachers who are working with children, dealing with children and grooming children, needs a special attention.

The reasons could be many, but during the study it was revealed that most of the teachers were not exposed to any training on CRC, for some it is very strange word to hear and some of them do not even reflect how they treat a child which is the necessary concern for them. There was no serious attempt made by any responsible authorities to give a meaningful training. Teachers never find the trainings important and to be implemented in their schools. Children are mostly taken for granted by the teachers and never show seriousness on children's issues and nowhere a child's views are paid attention.

Table 4.2: District wise Teachers Awareness on CRC in Percentage

Sl. No.	*Districts*	*High Awareness (%)*	*Low Awareness (%)*	*Total (%)*
1.	Hyderabad	28	72	100
2.	Ranga Reddy	18	82	100
3.	Mahabubnagar	25	75	100
4.	Medak	18	82	100
5.	Nalgonda	15.1	84.4	99
	Total	**20.8**	**79.1**	**100**

In all the districts included in the sample, most of the teachers have very low awareness Hyderabad (72%), Ranga Reddy (82%), Mahabubnagar (75%), Medak (82%), Nalgonda (84.4%). It is evident that only few teachers have awareness on CRC.

Table 4.3: Teachers Awareness on CRC

Teachers Awareness Level	*Percentage*
Low awareness on CRC	79.1
High awareness on CRC	20.8

Most of the teachers have less awareness (79.1%) and only some teachers (20.9%) have high awareness. i.e. the level of awareness in most of the teachers is very low. Also it is observed that the difference between the levels of awareness amongst teachers is found to be statistically significant. (Probability value 0.04)

In order to locate whether there is any influence of age, gender, qualification, type of management/type of school on the level of awareness a little intricate an analytical view is grappled here.

Teachers Awareness on CRC vs. Qualification

The results related to the awareness of teachers on CRC with respect to qualification presented in Table 4.4.

Table 4.4: Teachers Awareness on CRC *vs.* Qualification in Percentage

Qualification	*Low Awareness*	*Moderate Awareness*	*High Awareness*
UG	78.6	17.5	3.9
PG	80.0	15.5	4.5
M.Phil/Ph.D	60.0	20.0	20.0
Total	**79.2**	**16.4**	**4.4**

In order to really understand whether teachers qualification made any difference in their awareness related to children's rights, it is astonishing to observe that irrespective of their qualification most of the undergraduate teachers 180 (78.6%), post graduate 212 (80%), M.Phil/Ph.D qualified five (60%) have low level of awareness on child rights convention. Also statistically it is well represented that the difference is insignificant (Probability value is (.007).

Qualification did not make much significant difference in the awareness levels of teachers. On the whole awareness is low in teachers. Probably teachers never had any exposure to the child rights convention nor had an occasion to discuss except the ban on corporeal punishments in schools. But still we see many teachers are abusing, punishing and exploiting children in different contexts. It is witnessed in many reviews, news items and in media.

Teachers' Awareness on CRC vs. Gender

The results related to the awareness of teachers on CRC with respect to gender presented in Table 4.5.

Table 4.5: Teachers Awareness on CRC vs. Gender in Percentage

Gender	*Low Awareness*	*Moderate Awareness*	*High Awareness*
Male	85.2	11.1	3.7
Female	73.4	21.5	5.1
Total	**79.2**	**16.4**	**4.4**

Gender-wise also there is not much difference in the level of awareness of teachers on CRC. Most of the male 207 (85.2%), female 188 (73.4%) teachers have less awareness on child rights. A very few teachers (4.4%) show high awareness on child rights. However, the difference is significant statistically (Probability value 0.004).

Relatively most of the male teachers are less aware compared to female teachers. It could be basically due to the training programmes or otherwise participation in children's issues.

Mostly women teachers are given priority as they are represented as mother figures with emotional touch.

Teachers' Awareness on CRC vs. School Type

The results related to the awareness of teachers on CRC with respect to school type presented in Table 4.6.

Table 4.6: Teachers Awareness on CRC vs. School Type in Percentage

School Type	*Low Awareness*	*Moderate Awareness*	*High Awareness*	*Total*
Government	75.4	18.3	6.3	
Private	86.3	13.7	0	
Aided	100	0	0	
Total	**79.2**	**16.4**	**4.4**	

Only a few teachers 22 (6.3%) from Government schools show high level of awareness on child rights. Most of the Government schools 264 (75.4%), Private schools 113 (86.3%) and Aided 17 (100%) schools have less awareness on child rights. However, the difference between different managements is statistically significant (0.00 probability value). It is obvious that the training programmes conducted for few Government school teachers must have made a difference in their level of awareness when compared to private and aided schools.

It is observed in the field that most of the private school teachers are very harsh; insist on strict discipline. School managements also encourage harsh treatment and punish, humiliate children in various ways to get good score. Recent past news vindicate how a Lower Kindergarten (LKG) child was harshly punished by the teacher (*The Hindu* Newspaper, 2012). Similarly there are many such reviews which reveal this fact.

What are the Practices of Teachers in the Classroom

Most of the teachers (84.6%) encourage all categories of children to join in their schools. Teachers (89.4%) motivate children to come to school regularly and (67.1%) encourage children not to drop-out from the school. School teachers (88.8%) promote children in academics and to put up regular attendance. However, teachers (51.7%) feel that parents do not respond when they are called. Many teachers (86.6%) are worried about the children who are reluctant to come to school. Mostly teachers (82%) also encourage parents to send their children regularly to school.

Not many teachers (38.7%) are observant of children's problems. Parents and community oppose teachers (87.4%) when suggestions are extended by them. Some of the teachers (47.3%) give awareness to children who belong to low socio-economic background about benefits extended to them by the Government. More than half of the teachers (66.5%) strongly believe regularity and punctuality of children help in making teaching effective.

Mostly teachers (78.2%) never get bored with routine teaching and also they (64.5%) do not just go with lecture method. A good number of teachers (83.4%) use innovative methods in teaching. Teachers (80.6%) say that many children like to go with play-way method and project method. Only some teachers (45.3%) feel that classroom provides enriching experiences. Teachers (79.4%) said that they have adequate teaching-learning material. Only some teachers (33.7%) feel that the authorities should give the school good teaching-learning material. About half of the teachers (48.9%) cannot tolerate indiscipline in children. Also many teachers (79.4%) feel that extra freedom should not be given to children. Mostly (78.8%) teachers conduct remedial and special classes for slow learners.

Table 4.7: Practices of Teachers in their Classrooms in Percentage

Sl. No.	*Teachers Practices in Schools*	*Percentage*
1.	Teachers use innovative methods in teaching	83.40
2.	Teachers expressed child friendly methods are liked by children.	80.60
3.	Teacher conduct of remedial classes for slow learners.	79.40

The kind of practices which teachers reflected in their opinions gives a very colourful image about children's protection and positive child friendly approaches in their day to day school practices. Teachers are also keen to improve the schools for better facilities and practices.

The results related to awareness on child rights are annoying but does it really made a difference in their reflections on children's treatment and concern towards issues related to child rights protection.

4.2 How are the Facilities in the School?

Teachers feel that they have adequate facilities at their school. Teaching and

Table 4.8: Facilities in the School in Percentage

Sl. No.	*Adequate Facilities in the School*	*Percentage*
1.	Tg-Lg Material	63.5
2.	Physical facilities	57.3
3.	Classroom environment	70.3
4.	School premises	65.9
5.	Sanitary facilities	56.1
6	Training to teachers	74.1
7.	Learning experiences provided to children	59.1
8.	Extra-curricular activities	63.1

learning material; (63.5%), physical facilities (57.3%), classroom environment (70.3%), well maintained school premises (65.9%), sanitary facilities (56.1%), training provided to teachers (74.1%), learning experiences provided to children (59.1%) and extra-curricular activities (63.1%). Teachers who have responded could have been from the various schools where the facilities are provided. This also indicates that between 30-50 per cent of the schools do not possess adequate facilities. The situation could be due to government interventions wherever extended facilities could be adequate whereas in other schools facilities were not up to the mark.

It is obvious from the view of teachers about the various types of facilities and the teachers practices at the institution level and in the classroom are adequate which shows that more than half of the schools are child friendly suitable for children and teachers.

However, the remaining 30–40 per cent schools are not-child friendly. Probably, the kinds of reflections from different quarters of the society cited in different media belong to these schools.

Chapter 5
Children Perceptions on School Practices and Functioning

How do Children Perceive their School?

Sharp analytical views are captured to know children's perception on school practices and functioning. Many cases, reported through media on children, project that children are subjected to atrocities, made to commit suicides and they are abused, exploited physically, mentally, socially and emotionally even by their own parents and near and dear people.

> How horrifying to look at a headline that 'man kills his baby girl'....
> Man abandoned wife for giving birth to a baby girl....
> A School girl attempts suicide....
>> Why children in the early adolescent (Class X) need to commit suicide by jumping from the school building?

These are the indicators of status of child's protection. Such stories will never reveal the hidden reasons. We just read it as a news item, some of us react to it, reflect on it, a very few may be proactive in projecting and trying for justice.

Results Observed—How children perceive about their schools

How do Children Perceive about their Schools?

It is very annoying to note almost all aspects related to the schools were found to be statistically significant for most of the children's perception. Children felt that the furniture (88.8%), teaching learning material (88.8%), space (87.2%) in their classroom is adequate. Children (87%) feel that their school environment is maintained well and surroundings are kept clean.

Table 5.1: Children's Perception on School

Sl. No.	*Children's perception on school*	*Percentage Yes %*
1.	The furniture is adequate	88.8%
2.	Teaching learning material is adequate	88.8%
3.	Space in their classroom is adequate	87.2%
4.	Their school environment is maintained well and surroundings are kept clean.	87%
5.	Safe drinking water facility is not available in their school.	34.2%
6.	Schools do not provide adequate sanitary facilities to children.	46.9%
7.	Toilets are not maintained well	49.7%
8.	Health camps are not held in their schools.	36.7%

Some (34.2%) children feel that safe drinking water facility is not available in their school. Almost half (46.9%) of the schools do not provide adequate sanitary facilities to children. Almost equal number of children (49.7%) said they are not even maintained well. Some children (36.7%) said the health camps are not held in their schools.

Table 5.2: Children's Perception about their Teachers

Sl. No.	*Children's Perception about their teachers*	*Percentage*
1.	Teachers monitor health problems and guide the children	81.60%
2.	Teachers are very friendly in the classroom	84.70%
3.	Teachers come regularly to the class	81.60%
4.	Teachers absent themselves	32.70%
5.	Teachers treats children equally irrespective of their background	94.6
6.	Teachers encourage all children to participate in all activities	90.10%
7.	Teachers help slow learners and children from low socio-economic backgrounds.	89.80%
8.	Teachers are caring and concerned about each and every child.	90.80%
9.	Teachers teach very clearly	92.30%
10.	Teachers teach very interestingly	88%
11.	Audio-visual aids are used by teachers	74.70%
12.	Teachers motivate children to come to schools.	90.60%
13.	Teachers use abusive words or language	30.60%
14.	Teachers are favourable to some children	98.50%
15.	Teachers like children who are smart, rich and from high socio-economic background	22.20%
16.	Teachers punish children very badly	27.80%
17.	Teachers beat up children regularly	32.90%
18.	Teachers are cooperative with each other	87.20%
19.	Teachers are cooperative with children	91.80%
20.	Teachers are cooperative with parents	90.60%
21.	Teachers are cooperative with community	90.30%
22.	Teachers help children whenever required.	92.30%

Children (81.6%) feel that the teachers monitor health problems and guide the children. Children (84.7%) feel that teachers are very friendly in the classroom and most of the children (81.6%) said that teachers come regularly to the class. Only some children (32.7%) said teachers absent themselves. It is very encouraging to note that children (94.6%) expressed that all children are treated by the teachers equally irrespective of their background. Teachers (90.1%) encourage all children to participate in all the school activities.

Most of the children (89.8%) express their feeling that teachers help slow learners and children from low socio-economic background. Children (90.8%) feel that teachers are caring and concerned about each and every child. Most of the children perceived that teachers teach very clearly (92.3%), interestingly (88%) and use audio-visual aids (74.7%) in the class. Many children (90.6%) say that teachers motivate children to come to school regularly. Some children (30.6%) said that teachers use abusive words or language. Almost half of the children (48.5%) said teachers are favourable to some children. Some children (22.2%) also said teachers like those children who are smart, rich and from high socio-economic background. Some of the children (27.8%) said that teachers punish children very badly and (32.9%) said that teachers beat up children regularly.

Most of the children said teachers are cooperative with each other (87.2%), cooperative with children (91.80%), cooperative with parents (90.6%), cooperative with community (90.3%). Children (92.3%) also said teachers help children whenever required.

The positive perception of children could be due to the fear of adult world and they are used to the socially acceptable responses and act generally. During informal discussions and observations, children reveal their real and spontaneous expressions, where they say, if we do not do the homework, come irregularly to school or such of the instances, teacher will punish them.

On the whole it is very obvious in children's perception that schools are functioning well with adequate facilities.

What are the Real Stories Children Say?

Children's Perceptions of Teachers: A Closer View

Open ended questions were given to children to know about the popular teachers in their school. Which teacher children like the most and why? How do they expect a teacher to be? Various responses were collected from children from different districts. By and large children's feelings and expectation look similar.

The following themes were evolved after qualitative analysis of data:

1. Popular/child friendly teachers

2. Expectations about teachers
3. Memorable experiences of children
   i. positive
   ii. Negative
4. Parental relations
5. Suggestions to be child friendly School

1. Popular/Child Friendly Teachers

There are some popular teachers in each school. For various reasons either they teach well, treat well or show more concern for children who are regular to school.It is very obvious that some teachers impact children and remain popular amongst children and they influence them. They are loved and respected by most of the children out of the way as child friendly teachers.

"Those teachers are popular who teach well, teach interestingly, explain well, they understand well, they give examples, and give day to day examples, they create interest in the lesson, teach clearly, teach morals and etiquette in behaviour, special attention to slow learners, be friendly, helpful for children in their work, show concern for their health and other matters, give additional material like pens, books, etc. teach with experimentation and demonstration, give good marks, help in getting good marks, give chance to participate in all the programmes, conduct competitions, make them to play promote interpersonal skills, treat like parents, teach manners, morals, guidance and give suggestions, correct children's misdeeds, take them out for exhibitions and fairs, help in solving personal problems, kind and helpful, unwavering support, teach religious values (to pray every day), behave well with children, teach with audio-visual material, teach unknown and new things.

Holistically, children like those teachers with good proficiency in subject and those teach well and teachers who are good and friendly and show concern towards children, yet at times children won't mind if teachers are little strict and punish them, if required. Mostly children like teacher with good subject and good personality.

What children say? *"My teachers are good, patient and tolerant do not show any tiredness and repeat lessons till we understand and satisfied.". "I am scared of PT sir because he beats us. "My teachers beat and scold if we do not read. If we get less marks my teachers threaten us". "When we do not do homework or commit any mistake my teachers scold and beat us.". "I fear my HM because he is always serious." "Those children, who have bad habits, show bad mannerism are beaten and scolded by the teachers, so we like our teachers." "Even though he is strict, he teaches well so I like my teacher. I want to listen to him any number of times.*

Mostly children feel that they understand what teachers teach and whenever they do not teach clearly they ask questions. Teachers allow us to ask questions related to academics.

It shows children like those teachers who are child-friendly. Similarly, children like such teachers who teach well and behave well with children who focus on many interesting life stories relevant to the text book stories. Teachers who solve children's personal problems are liked by children.

The child likes the teacher who maintains good intimate relation with them, give opportunity to participate and inspire them to reach new heights and settle well in their life.

"*Very rarely teachers beat us, but when we behave extremely, they punish us. Some teachers restrict girl students to behave in a particular way". "Girls should bend their heads while walking".*

Most of the children want their teachers to be

"*like a friend, parent, humorous, joyful, cooperative, guide them, accompany them not only in the class but also while playing. Teachers should love every child, should encourage the children to share their problems. Teachers should show concern, and they should encourage children to study and play accordingly. When children do not study, teachers should try to understand their problems and help them. Teachers should be like their family members".*

Children want teachers to be

"*friendly, intimate, free, understand, guide and be like their family members". They do not like teachers who beat, shout, strict, speak with loud voice, harsh, not intimate, put them to fear and serious*".

2. Expectations About Teachers

A child expects a teacher to:

"*Teach students very clearly, use effectively all gadgets and technology, guide them. Celebrate all national days, festivals in the school, take them for field trips, outings, tours and enjoy with children like friends. Treat everybody equally, encourage them to learn and make efforts to get through the SSC examination. Encourage children to ask questions, give freedom and maintain good relations with children. When it is necessary, I will be little harsh and punish them mildly.*"

Teachers should "do their duty properly and dutifully". "*If I become a teacher, I will teach English to every Indian child from Urdu medium*". "*I will try to understand their feelings and encourage them in all aspects*". "*I will motivate, encourage, give freedom, move closely and make them successful in their examination*". "*I will not punish children*"

"They should teach clearly, understandably, interestingly with teaching aids, clarify doubts, should teach at a low pace speed, through experiments, technology, practical experiences, field experiences with examples and explain dramatically".

"They should be well dressed, regular, punctual, teach properly to all children. They want their teachers to teach lesson like a story. Teachers should teach the lesson by analyzing critically, logically, analytically. They should get engrossed and involved while teaching".

3. Memorable experiences shared by children

Mostly they say about day to day events they experience like farewell day, school days, national festivals, good facilities, self-governance, whenever they get appreciation.

Positive experiences: *"When I get high score everybody clapped for me, when I gave a speech on Republic Day, everybody appreciated me". We cannot forget the memories of field trips and tours". When I received a prize in competition". "Children treat teachers like a God".*

"Children like those incidences which motivate them, benefit them, give chance to express their views, participate in different events, enjoy and celebrations, etc. They love to celebrate and enjoy the events, innovative and new ways of teaching in the classroom".

Facilities: Children like and feel happy about the facilities in their school, "Good facilities, computers, playground, good library books, school ambience, good marks, punctuality, science lab, digital classroom, mineral water, big trees and shade, good sanitary facilities, good quotes are shared, good friends and teachers"

Children like friends who are good, who share and are polite and helpful to others.

Some children have very good rapport with friends and they say we are good friends.

Some children say if we move freely teachers misunderstand. Mostly children feel that their friends are good and they never correlate friendship with studies.

Negative experiences: *"When I could not meet the teacher's expectations, teacher was annoyed and scolded me. I cannot forget that in my lifetime".*

My bad memory in life! "*When I was in Class I, I used to run away from school and go home and sleep. I used to do it daily. But one day I wanted to go home so I went to Sir and told him that I want to go to toilet and he allowed me. One of the student saw me going home instead of going toilet. Next day, when I sought my Sir's permission to go for toilet, my Sir took my slate and beat me very badly with it. I got angry and I used very bad language, my Sir got annoyed he lifted me up and threw me down. I can never forget this. Children cannot forget even painful events like teachers' treatment, scolding, punishment, etc".*

Many children shared the facilities that they lack in their schools like:

"We do not have good playground, teachers should be there for all subjects, we sit in verandah we do not have classrooms, we sit under the tree, our school strength is very less, girls have no toilets. We do not have good facilities and no toilets. There are no fans, we feel hot. We have no glass panes to windows, no lights. We want a smart board. Adequate classrooms are not available, we have lab but rarely used".

"When the friends do not talk/fight". "A disabled child feels very painful when all other children play". "When they fail or score lesser and teachers punish". Whenever loving teachers get transferred or retire from their service, children feel pain and cannot tolerate. "I failed in English subject and I felt very bad and decided to study well". "When my classmate died". "When my classmate went for swimming and drowned". "When an old person fell and got hurt in front of our gate". Children expressed their concern.

"When children go away with child-marriage tradition unexpectedly, it is painful for children". "When teacher makes children sit in hot sun as a punishment, I do not like". "If teacher punishes any children I cannot bear and I feel very bad". "I study well and write my exam well, even then teacher beats me". Children sing songs on gender issues while playing skits representing the role of girls". Children cried at that time when . . other children are injured.

One of my classmate got hurt with bell in eye, I felt very painful.

Mostly children say socially acceptable answers/responses. However, some children say that they do not like some of their teachers. Some teachers are praised as they teach well. Children also express that teachers should treat everybody equally.

"My teachers should come to school regularly. I don't like when teachers take care of one student and do not care for other students." "My teacher is like God."My teachers and HM (Head Master) beat up openly, no parent ask them. We do not have teachers for some subjects. Our school arranges tuitions which is mandatory."

In few schools teachers just come to school for the sake of salary, they do not take classes, they sit in the staff room and read newspaper. Some teachers think even if we take class or not, Government will pay us salary every month. But in our school "*our teachers are different, they take classes regularly and make us understand what they teach and always encourage us. We want our teachers to make us bright, dynamic/vibrant*". We want them to be loving, friendly with us. Most children feel teachers are good and helpful and concerned about children, however, yet they punish them at times.

4. Parental Relations

"My parents are very good they provide us everything. They forego one meal every day to feed us three times daily. They encourage us to study to become great. Parents do not encourage watching TV and wasting time". Some children say that their parents want them to get married but the children do not like it. "Our parents work very hard to make us study. They feel that we should stand on our own feet and become independent". 'I want to become a lawyer and do justice to the society.' "My parents cannot bear if we have any problem."

Most of the parents of the children studying in the Government schools are uneducated, daily labourers and migrants.

"Children feel that their parents should take care of their education and come to school and meet the teachers to know about their progress." "My parents say that they will continue my studies if I pass SSC otherwise get me married." 'I like to go to college and I like to study' (she works as a maid and studying in eighth standard). *"I am proud to be born to my parents. By looking at their economic status, I feel pity to ask anything for my health."*

5. Suggestions to Become Child Friendly School

"We should have greenery around, teacher should be friendly, class strength should be good and we need to have adequate physical facilities. Teachers should teach well and should get a good name to school. Teachers should not fight among themselves. School should have security–our school bell was stolen. Outside our school, there is a graveyard, we get bad smell and some children become sick, we need good surroundings, we have no gate, thus animals enter into school and spoil the plants that we grow. Our HM or villagers do not bother about it".

There should be laboratory, good lighting. Children have no discipline they make hell of a noise. Many students are irregular in our school.

We have no English teacher; we should have teachers to teach every subject. They make hell of a noise. Many students are irregular in our school. We need more teachers, when teachers do not come, students look after the class. Some teachers teach well, some do not teach well. There is a need for good sanitary facilities. We need separate toilets for girls and boys. We should have running water in toilets.

Every week at least once we should have games / sports period. We want a good play ground. Every month at least one plant should be planted in the school premises and surroundings.

Teachers should maintain good discipline and inculcate good manners in children. School environment should be green. Children should not tease teachers but learn to respect them. Mid-day meal provided in school is not good or tasty. All students should be encouraged to take part in all the activities. Teachers should promote creativity in children. School should be environment friendly. Our school should be neat, tidy and green. Teachers should understand children's problems. My teachers are good, it is our good luck, should show the way to life. School should have regular white wash, nothing should be written on school walls, window panes should be there.

Some children say they have good facilities. However, about 30-40% schools need to be equipped with physical amenities and facilities. Teachers should promote creativity in children.

My wish is to do some great help to school which should be memorable forever.

I lost my father when I was a child. My mother is working in a small company for the family survival, as we are financially weak we also should work hard and we get very little time to study. Our teachers are little strict. We need more teachers in our school. A little classroom cleanliness is required, games should be improved.

Chapter 6

Existing Status, Facilities and Teacher Practices

Observations

The reports on children rights protection in the media are discouraging and dismaying, while the results from the study show a different picture where the children are treated well in most of the schools in all the aspects.

Treatment of children in the school by their teachers was observed in five dimensions by the investigator. Where ever necessary some responses were collected from the teachers.

1. Physical Dimension
2. Psychological/Emotional Dimension
3. Sexual Dimension
4. Cultural/Social Dimension
5. Health, Hygiene, Nutrition Dimension

Physical Dimension

The results related to physical dimension are presented below:

Table 6.1: Physical Dimension

Sl. No.	*Physical Dimension*	*Percentage*	
		No	*Yes*
1.	Hitting/beating with cane physically	90.70	9.3
2.	Physical injury	95.7	4.3
3.	Physical punishment	94.3	5.7
4.	Man handling	97.1	2.9

The study reveals that teachers treat children without hurting physically (90.7%), children are not hurt physically through physical punishment (95.7%), they are not physically punished (94.3%), and they are not man handled (97.1%). This indicates that in many schools teachers are very child-friendly and treat children well. A very negligible (2.5%) number of teachers abuse and punish children physically.

Psychological and Emotional Dimension

The results related to psychological dimension are presented below:

Table 6.2: Psychological and Emotional Dimension

Sl. No.	*Psychological and Emotional Dimension*	*Percentage*
1.	No feeling of shame	95.0
2.	Do not ridicule children	95.7
3.	Do not create fear	80.0
4.	Children are not threatened	82.9
5.	Children not put to humiliation, shame, distress and pain	95.0
6.	Do not segregate in the school or class	95.7
7.	Do not show any indifference in their attitude towards children	95.7
8.	Teachers are friendly and do not dominate on any child	92.1
9.	Show keen interest and personal attention towards children by caring and without any kind of neglect	95.7
10.	Never put them to ill-treatment	95.7
11.	No fear of their teachers	83.6
12.	Express happiness	94.3

It is very encouraging to note that teachers do not attempt to create any feeling of shame (95.0%). They don't use any insulting words or ridicule children (95.7%). Mostly, teachers (80%) do not create fear in children through their behaviour or body language. Only some (20%) of the schools are creating fear through their behaviour and body language and other expressions. In most of the schools (82.9%) children are not threatened by the teachers regarding the consequences they have to face for their various acts in the school. Even children are not put to humiliation, shame, distress and pain (95%) by their teachers in the classroom.

Teachers treat all the children equally without any discrimination and do not isolate them from the group and also do not segregate in the school or class activities they conduct (95.7%). Mostly teachers are very good and mingle with them and do not show any indifference (95.7%) in their attitude towards children. Many teachers are friendly and do not dominate on any child (92.1%). Teachers also show keen interest and personal attention towards children by caring and without any kind of neglect (95.7%).

Teachers (95.7%) treat the children properly even during the assembly, in the class and in the school and they are never put them to ill-treatment. In majority of schools teacher gives freedom to children and they have no fear of their teachers and are always ready to speak freely and express themselves (83.6%).

No way, a child looked unhappy in the school or morrows or sad. Most of the children (94.3%) express happiness about their school. The results show that children are psychologically and emotionally comfortable and they are happy and go well with their teachers and the school. On the whole this reveals that most of the teachers and schools are child-friendly.

Sexual Dimension

The results related to sexual dimension are presented below:

Table 6.3: Sexual Dimension

Sl. No.	Sexual Dimension	Percentage
1.	Do not tolerate any kind of sexual abuse	96.4
2.	Misbehaving	97.1
3.	Subjecting their feelings	95.0
4.	Enforce to be with them	97.1
5.	Calling children home	97.9
6	Targeting in different ways related to dress and other aspects.	92.9

Almost 95-97 per cent of the teachers do not trouble the children either by exploiting them sexually or by ill-treating or take advantage of their behaviour and actions, but teachers act as an elderly soothing person. It was reported by the children that teachers and other members never misbehave or abuse sexually. As such, the teachers do not tolerate any kind of sexual abuse (96.4%), misbehaving (97.1%), subjecting their feelings (95%), enforce to be with them (97.1%), calling children home (97.9%), targeting in different ways related to dress and other aspects (92.9%).

It was observed that only few schools 2-3 per cent, where teachers put the children to discomfort. But otherwise, children are sexually protected by the teachers and comforted in the schools through their attitude, behaviour and their approach towards treating children with all concern.

Cultural and Social Dimension

Generally teachers do not interfere or target the children with respect to their habits, social customs or cultural practices. Teachers do not put any restriction on dress pattern of girls (80.2%), do not discriminate girls (95%), do not insist on any specific dress pattern (86.4%), except for uniform which is also relaxed many times to encourage children to come to school.

However, some teachers (30-40%) are very particular and insist that at least some social and cultural norms to be observed by girl students. They are firm on certain behaviour related to eating (38.6%), while playing (32.9%), talking/interacting with boys (42.1%), and sitting postures (31.4%).

It is observed that some teachers are still keen on restricting or curtailing the freedom of children and expect them to behave in a particular way. Still teachers for various reasons restrict girl's behaviour and direct them to be in a particular way.

Table 6.4: Restriction on Girls: Cultural and Social Dimensions

Sl. No.	*Restriction on Girls—Cultural and Social dimensions*	*Percentage*	
		Yes	*No*
i.	While eating	38.60	61.40
ii.	While playing	32.90	67.10
iii.	While talking to or interacting with boys	57.90	42.10
iv.	While sitting	68.60	31.40
v.	Teacher takes example related to cultural practice	24.30	75.70
vi.	Teacher insist specific habits, values and practices	33.60	66.40

i. While eating, girls are expected to be:

Girls are expected to follow approved way of eating culture. Girls are directed while eating to eat as per their approved practices in the respective school social and cultural context. Some teachers feel in some schools (38.6%) that girls need to follow such norms.

ii. While playing, girls are expected to be:

Some teachers insist on girls to follow certain ways while playing (32.9%), which clearly seen that teachers show a discriminatory attitude towards girls.

iii. While talking to or interacting with boys, girls are expected to be:

Almost in half of the schools teachers insist on girls' behaviour while talking to boys or interacting with boys in a particular way (42.1%). In one co-education school, teachers and HM together took a decision to keep all the girls in one section and boys in the other section in order to avoid certain untoward problems which otherwise observed by the teachers in school campus in some ZPHS schools.

iv. While sitting, girls are expected to be:

Almost 1/3rd of the schools (31.4%) teachers insist on children to follow a particular way of sitting in the classroom or otherwise.

v. Teacher takes examples related to cultural practice

Some of the teachers in the schools (24.3%) take culture specific examples. This may hurt the children belonging to that group and lead to certain problem in the classroom and may also give rise to grave consequences. In a way this is an act against the children's rights.

vi. Teacher insist specific habits, values and practices

The specific habits, values, practices are insisted by the teachers to follow. 1/3rd of the teachers (33.6%) insist on children to follow certain specific habits, values and practices. It may curtail the freedom of the children in terms of their practice and expression. Basic child rights and minimum things are not given by the teachers.

Most of the teachers (97.1%) do not hurt or abuse children belonging to specific caste and also do not refer to their practices as good or bad or not etiquette or uncultured and so forth. Majority of teachers (97.1%) do not hurt children belonging to lower community groups or insult by pin-pointing them. Teachers (7.1%) find fault with the language the children use and correct them with the approved dominant language accent and some teachers (24.3%) specifically take the examples from dominant cultural practices. About 1/3rd of the teachers insist children to follow specific habits, values and practices.

Health Dimension

The results related to health dimension are presented below:

Table 6.5: Teachers Concern about Children Health

Sl. No.	Teachers concern about children health	Percentage
1.	Teachers talk to children and explain about the health	98.60
2.	Vaccination through health camps	77.10
3.	Schools conduct regular health checkups	75.0
4.	No PMC in school vicinity	22.90
5.	No health workers in the PHC	28.60
6.	Teachers pay attention to children health problems	95.70

Most of the schools take care of the health aspects of the children. Teachers in many schools (98.6%) talk to children and clearly explain about the healthcare. Mostly (77.1%) schools provide vaccination to children through regular health camps. About 1/4th (25%) of the schools do not have regular health checkups for children, this shows 1/3rd of the schools do not conduct the health camps, but the remaining children are not paid attention in terms of their health condition. About 1/4th (22.9%) of schools do not have primary health centre in their vicinity which indicates the non-availability or access to the health facilities for many children in rural areas. To the extent of 1/3rd (28.6%) primary health centres do not have the presence of health workers.

Majority of the teachers (95.7%) in schools pay immediate attention to children suffering from any health problem. This shows that the teachers are concerned about children's health issues.

Hygiene Practices

The results related to hygiene practices are presented below:

Table 6.6: Hygiene Practices in the School

Sl. No	*Hygiene Practices in the School*	*Percentage*
1.	Dustbins are not present in classroom	80.00
2.	School premises used as dumping waste	67.90
3.	No mechanism for regular disposal of the waste	87.10
4.	Schools do not have toilets	50.70
5.	Separate toilet for girls are not available	47.9
5.	No water, buckets, mugs in the toilets	41.40
6.	No scavenging facilities	62.90
7.	Toilets are not cleaned and maintained regularly	38.60
8.	Teachers insist children to wear neat uniform	75.0

It is very obvious to note that the hygienic practices in most of the schools are discouraging. Majority of schools do not pay much attention towards up-keep of their classrooms and school premises. It is evident that in most of the classrooms (80%) dustbins are not seen. More than half of the schools (67.9%) made their premises as dumping place for waste. Most of the (87.1%) schools do not have a mechanism for safe/regular disposal of the waste.

Sanitary Facilities in Schools

The results related to sanitary facilities are presented below:

Table 6.7: Sanitary Facilities in Schools

Sl. No.	*Sanitary Facilities*	*Percentage*
1.	No adequate toilets	50.7
2.	No separate toilets for girls and boys	47.9
3.	No sufficient water, buckets, mugs available	41.4
4.	No scavenging facilities	62.9
5.	Not cleaned regularly	38.6

It is also observed that almost half of the schools do not either have or if available do not maintain sanitary facilities. At least half of the schools 71 (50.7%) do not have adequate toilets. In almost half of the schools 76 (47.9%) separate toilets for girls and boys are not available. Similarly, there is no sufficient water, buckets, mugs available 62 (41.4%) in the toilets. Most of the 87(62.9%) schools do not have scavenging facilities, 53 (38.6%) toilets are not cleaned regularly or maintained cleanly.

This shows that most of the schools do not provide adequate sanitary facilities to children. The very basic biological necessity is not fulfilled when the child come to school. So, the big question is how long children will continue in the schools especially girls. However, 75 per cent teachers insist children to maintain personal hygiene and come to school with clean and neat uniform and wear hygienic clothes and teachers work towards welfare of the child. Many teachers said in informal talks that the teachers contribute much on their own and privately appoint somebody for cleaning toilets. In some schools children in turns clean the classrooms.

Nutrition

The results related to nutrition are presented below:

Table 6.8: Nutrition and Healthy Practices in the School

Sl. No	*Nutrition*	*Percentage*
1.	Teachers monitor mid-day meals	79.30
2.	Schools do not pay attention to mid-day meals	33.60
3.	Teachers promote nutritional values in the food	77.90
4.	Teachers give awareness on healthy nutritional diet	85.00
5.	Surroundings kept clean where food is served	76.40

About 3/4th of the children in schools look healthy in their physical appearance. Probably the children may be well nourished by their parent's and also by the midday meals in the schools

In most of the schools (79.3%) teachers monitor mid-day meals and show interest towards children's food, eating mannerism and etiquette is maintained by the children during midday meals. About 1/3rd of the schools (33.6%) do not pay attention to midday meals quality. Mostly (77.9%) teachers promote nutritional values in the food. Many teachers (85%) give awareness on healthy practices and nutritional diet. Many schools (76.4%) keep the surroundings clean where the food is served. About 1/3rd of the schools show less interest and do not pay much attention and neglect the important areas related to nutrition.

Child Friendly Practices in Schools

Will there be any difference in being child friendly with respect to the teachers qualification, age, gender, teaching subject, school locality, school type, and so on....?

School Facilities: Types of Schools

The results related to school facilities in different types of schools are presented below:

Table 6.9: Type of School *vs.* Child Friendly Practices

School Type	*More Child Friendly Percentage*	*Less Child Friendly Percentage*
Government	92.7	7.3
Private	90.0	10.0
Total	**90.2**	**9.8**

Most of the private 27 (90%) and Government 102 (92.7%) schools and teachers appear to be child friendly in overall aspects of the school. Probably the recent past interventions by the Government in a way must have provided the physical building and facilities, recruitment of teachers and other dimensions.

School Facilities with Respect to Locality

The results related to school facilities in different locality are presented below:

Table 6.10: School Facilities with Respect to Locality *vs.* Child Friendly Practices

Locality	*More child friendly Percentage*	*Less child friendly Percentage*
Urban	92.8	7.2
Rural	92.1	7.9
Total	**92.2**	**7.8**

Irrespective of the locality urban 13 (92.8%) and rural 116 (92.1%) are child friendly in overall aspects of the school practices.

Teachers Qualification vs. Child Friendly Practices

Table 6.11: Teachers Qualification *vs.* Child Friendly Practices

Qualification	*More Child Friendly Percentage*	*Less Child Friendly Percentage*
UG	92.4	7.6
PG	91.4	8.6
M. Phil/Ph.D	100.0	0
Total	**92.1**	**7.9**

Higher the qualification of teachers more child friendly are the schools practices. All the Ph.D qualified 4 (100%), PG 64 (91.4%) and UG 61 (92.4%) are more child friendly.

Teaching Subjects vs. Child Friendly Practices

Table 6.12: Teaching Subject *vs.* Child Friendly Practices

Teaching Subject	*More child friendly Percentage*	*Less child friendly Percentage*
Telugu	88.8	11.2
Hindi	100.0	0
English	90.9	9.1
Mathematics	88.0	12.0
Bio.Sc,/Phy.Sc	90.4	9.6
Social Studies	90.4	9.6
Physical Education	100.0	0
Computer	100.0	0
Total	**90.2**	**9.8**

Almost all the teachers with different subjects: Telugu 24 (88.8%), Hindi 11 (100%), English 20 (90.9%), Mathematics 22 (88.0%), Biological Science and Physical Science 34 (90.4%), Social studies 16 (90.4%), Physical education 1 (100%), Computer 1 (100 %) are observed to be more child friendly.

Teacher Age vs. Child Friendly Practices (*see* Table 6.13)

Almost all age group teachers Low 1 (100%), Moderate 87 (64.0%) and High 48 (35.3%) are more child friendly in their appearance and practices and in functioning of the school.

Table 6.13: Teacher Age *vs.* Child Friendly Practices

Teacher Age	*More Child Friendly*	*Less Child Friendly*	*Total*
Low	100	0	
Moderate	89.77	19.33	
High	96.0	4.0	

Teaching Experience vs. Child Friendly Practices

Majority of the teachers with different years of experience up to five years 34 (26.4%), 6-10 years 26 (20.1%), 11-15 years 38 (29.5%), 16 and above 31 (24.0%) are more child friendly in functioning and practices. This may be because of various mandates and policy matters like ban on corporal punishment, qualitative improvement of schools through SSA and so on could have created such child friendly ambience and functioning on the whole.

Table 6.14: Teaching Experience vs. Child Friendly Practices

Teaching Experience	*More Child Friendly Percentage*	*Less Child Friendly Percentage*
Less than 5 yrs	26.4	9.0
6-10 yrs	20.1	18.0
11-15 yrs	29. 5	54.0
16 and above	24.0	19.0

Gender vs. Child Friendly Practices

Male 71 (55.0%) and female 58 (45.0%) teachers are more child friendly. Gender did not make much difference in being child friendly. Irrespective of gender, almost all the teachers are child-friendly.

Table 6.15: Gender vs. Child Friendly Practices

Gender	*More Child Friendly*	*Less Child Friendly*
Male	55.0	82.0
Female	45.0	18.0

It is very interesting and encouraging to note from the results that almost all the schools investigators observed their functioning on overall dimensions found to be more child-friendly.

This clearly shows that teachers are more concerned and are good to children. A noteworthiness of the schools is being more child-friendly practices. There are very few schools which found to be less child-friendly in overall dimensions.

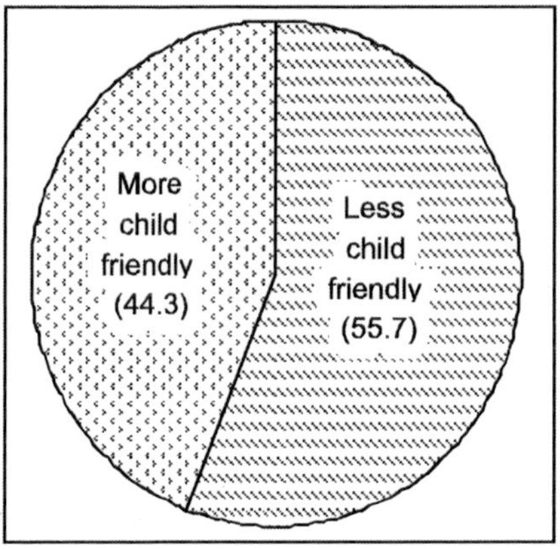

Fig. 6.16: Hygiene *vs.* Child Friendly Practices

In almost all the dimensions schools appear to be child friendly, however, with respect to hygiene dimension it was found that almost half of the schools are more child friendly in their practices 62 (44.3%).

Chapter 7

How Far Schools are Child Friendly?

School Facilities

It is hard to note that only two (3.2%) schools at Medak have excellent facilities. Also it is noted that the facilities are good at only one (1.6%), at average level 11 (17.7%) schools. The remaining schools where 31 (50%) are poor and 17 (27.4%) in their very poor facilities.

On the whole it is observed that more than 50 per cent schools are with below average level school facilities.

Table 7.1: School Facilities in Five Districts of Andhra Pradesh

Facilities	*Frequency*	*Percentage*
Very Poor	17	27.4
Poor	31	50.0
Average	11	17.7
Good	1	1.6
Excellent	2	3.2
Total	**62**	**100.0**

Except Medak two (3.2%) schools, remaining all other districts, there are no schools with excellent school facilities in other four districts—Ranga Reddy, Hyderabad, Nalgonda and Mahaboobnagar.

School Building

School Building at a Glance (*see* Fig. on next page)

Excellent School Buildings

Average School Buildings

Poor School Buildings

School Building with Respect to Type of School and Locality

The results related to type of the schools, the locality and the status of the building shown in Table 7.2.

Table 7.2: Type of School *vs.* School Building

School Type	*Very Poor*	*Poor*	*Average*	*Excellent*	*Total*
	No. (%)	*No. (%)*	*No. (%)*	*No. (%)*	*No.*
Government	15 (29.5%)	24 (47.0%)	10 (19.6%)	2 (3.92%)	51
Private	5 (45.5%)	5 (45.5%)	1 (9.09%)	0	11
Total	**20**	**29**	**11**	**2**	**62**

In private schools the school building—five (45.5%) poor, five (45.5%) very poor and in Government schools—15 (29.5%) very poor and 24 (47.0%) poor. None of the private school buildings are excellent.

Table 7.3: Locality *vs.* School Building

Locality	Very Poor	Poor	Average	Excellent	Total
	No. (%)	No. (%)	No. (%)	No. (%)	No. (%)
Urban	8 (58.0%)	6 (43.0%)	0	0	14
Rural	12 (25.0 %)	23 (47.91%)	11 (22.91%)	2 (4.1%)	48
Total	**20**	**29**	**11**	**2**	**62**

All the schools selected in the sample observed six (43.0%) poor and eight (58.0%) very poor in urban and 12 (25.0 %) very poor, 23 (47.91%) poor in rural localities. None of the schools in urban area have excellent school building.

Schools Facilities District Wise, Locality and Type of School

How is the Space in the School Building?

Table 7.4: District-wise Space in the School Building

District	Very Poor No. (%)	Poor No. (%)	Average No. (%)	Good No. (%)	Excellent No. (%)	Total
Ranga Reddy	0	11 (100%)	0	0	0	11
Hyderabad	2 (20.0%)	5 (50.0%)	3 (30%)	0	0	10
Medak	4 (27.0%)	5 (33.3%)	3 (20.0%)	1 (6.6%)	2 (13.33%)	15
Nalgonda	1 (9.0%)	9 (82.0%)	1 (9.0%)	0	0	11
Mahaboobnagar	1 0 (66.7%)	1 (6.7%)	4 (27.0%)	0	0	15
Total	**17**	**31**	**11**	**1**	**2**	**62**

The situation with respect to the building space in the schools of five districts is not at all encouraging except Medak. In Medak only one school has good space, two schools are excellent in space, and in remaining all other districts, no school has either adequate or more than adequate space in the building. Most of the schools are poor and very poor in the building space. In Ranga Reddy district: 11 (100 %) poor; Hyderabad: poor five (50%); average three (30%); very poor two (20%). Medak: very poor four (26.6 %); poor five (33.3%); average three (20.0%); good one (6.6 %), excellent two (13.33). Nalgonda: very poor one (9.0%); poor nine (82.0%), average one (9.0%).

Mahaboobnagar: very poor 10 (66.7%), poor one (6.7%), average four (27.0%).

From the above results it is very clear that most of the schools do not have adequate space in the building which reflects that the schools do not provide sufficient space for children as per the prescribed norms. It shows that schools are not child-friendly. No private school has excellent space or good space in the building except one is good and two are excellent in terms of building space in Government schools, remaining schools are mostly poor and very poor.

No urban school is with good or excellent building space. Only few are good and two excellent in space in rural schools. On the whole most of the schools are with poor and very poor building space.

Are the schools provided with well aerated buildings?

Table 7.5: District-wise Aeration in School Building

Districts	*Very Poor (%)*	*Poor (%)*	*Average (%)*	*Good (%)*
Ranga Reddy	9.09	73	18.18	0
Hyderabad	30.00	70	0	0
Medak	20.00	60	3.3	1
Nalgonda	18.00	73	9	0
Mahaboobnagar	73.40	0	26.6	0
Total	**32.25**	**51.6**	**14.51**	**1.61**

None of the schools in five districts have excellent aeration in the building. Only one school in Medak shows good aeration. Very few nine (14.51%) schools are at average and most of the schools in the five districts are poor 32 (51.6%) and very poor 20 (32.2%) in providing aeration.

Table 7.6: District-wise Ventilation

Districts	*Very Poor (%)*	*Poor (%)*	*Average (%)*
Ranga Reddy	9.09	63.63	27.27
Hyderabad	30	70	—
Medak	33.33	46.6	20
Nalgonda	18.18	63.63	18.18
Mahaboobnagar	73.3	—	26.6
Total	**35.4**	**45.16**	**19.35**

No school is ventilated excellently or even good amongst five districts. Some of the schools 12 (19.4%) are average i.e. partially ventilated. But majority of the schools are with poor 28 (45.5%) and very poor 22 (35.5%) ventilation. This shows that building in most of the schools are not properly ventilated i.e. it may in turn effect the children health and their growth and development which is not very child friendly.

Table 7.7: School Type *vs.* Ventilation

School Type	Very poor (%)	Poor (%)	Average (%)
Government	33.33	45.09	21.56
Private	45.45	45.45	9.1

Most of the Government and private schools are very poor and poorly ventilated.

Table 7.8: Locality *vs.* Ventilation

Locality	Very Poor (%)	Poor (%)	Average (%)
Urban	50.0	50.0	–
Rural	31.25	43.75	25.0
Total	**35.48**	**45.16**	**19.35**

All the schools located in urban are poor seven (50%) and very poor seven (50%). Most of the schools located in rural areas are with poor 21 (44.0%) and very poor 15 (31.0%) ventilation. On the whole ventilation in the schools is not up to the mark.

Space in the Classroom

Table 7.9: District Wise *vs.* Space in the Classroom

District	*Very Poor (%)*	*Poor (%)*	*Average (%)*	*Excellent (%)*
Ranga Reddy	–	100	–	–
Hyderabad	30.0	40.0	30.0	–
Medak	13.33	53.33	26.6	6.6
Nalgonda	9.09	90.9	–	–
Mahaboobnagar	73.33	6.66	20	–
Total	**27.41**	**54.83**	**16.1**	**1.61**

About 80 per cent of the schools (poor 54.8%, very poor 27.4%) do not have adequate space in the classrooms in almost all the districts.

Table 7.10: School Type *vs.* Space in the Classroom

School Type	*Very Poor* (%)	*Poor* (%)	*Average* (%)	*Excellent* (%)
Government	29.41	50.98	17.64	1.96
Private	18.18	72.72	9.09	–
Total	**27.4**	**54.8**	**22.8**	**6.7**

Only one school has excellent space in the classroom and nine (18%) are at average level but most of the schools are poor 26 (54%) and very poor 12 (25%) in Government schools. Even in the private schools the space in the classroom is not adequate. Either they are poor or very poor.

Table 7.11: Locality *vs.* Space in the Classroom

School Type	*Very Poor*	*Poor*	*Average*	*Excellent*
Urban	35.71	57.14	7.14	0
Rural	25.0	54.16	18.75	2.08
Total	**27.4**	**54.8**	**22.8**	**6.7**

Both in urban and rural areas most of the schools do not have adequate space in the classroom.

Table 7.12: District-wise School Ambience

District	*Very Poor* (%)	*Poor* (%)	*Average* (%)	*Excellent* (%)
RR	36.36	54.54	–	9.09
Hyderabad	30.0	60.0	10.0	–
Medak	20.0	40.0	26.66	13.33
Nalgonda	45.45	45.45	–	9.09
MBNR	73.33	6.66	20.0	–

School building ambience is also not properly maintained in almost all the schools in five districts except one school in Ranga Reddy, Nalgonda and two in Medak surroundings are neat and clean.

Table 7.13: District-wise Playground

District	*Very Poor (%)*	*Poor (%)*	*Average (%)*	*Excellent (%)*
RR	90.90	9.09	–	–
Hyderabad	60	40	–	–
Medak	66.66	26.66	–	6.66
Nalgonda	81.81	9.09	–	9.09
MBNR	80	–	20	–

Most of the schools do not have proper playground in the school premises. Only two schools in Nalgonda and Medak have good play ground in their schools. Without suitable or good playground, children's physical development gets affected. And also to conduct co-curricular activities it would be difficult without proper playground. Children love to play and it is necessary for children to play for their proper development. This is one of the indicators to describe a school as child-friendly. Children love to play and grow through play.

Play Ground in the Schools

Whether Children are Allowed to Play in the Schools?

Table 7.14: Children allowed to Play in the School

Allowed	*(%)*
Yes	87.1
No	12.9

Except a few schools eight (12.9%) all other schools allow children to play.

Table 7.15: School Type *vs.* Children are Allowed to Play

School Type	*Yes (%)*	*No (%)*	*Total (%)*
Govt.	84.31	15.68	82.25
Private	100.0	–	17.74

Most of the schools—both Government and private—in rural and urban localities allow children to play (87%).

Table 7.16: District-wise Adequate Furniture

District	*Very Poor (%)*	*Poor (%)*	*Average (%)*	*Good (%)*	*Excellent (%)*
Ranga Reddy	81.81	18.18	0	0	0
Hyderabad	100.0	0	0	0	0
Medak	46.66	26.66	13.33	6.66	6.66
Nalgonda	100.0	–	–	–	–
MBNR	86.66	13.33	–	–	–
Total	**80.64**	**12.90**	**3.22**	**1.61**	**1.61**

Most of the schools in five districts (80.6%) do not have adequate furniture and the condition is very poor in these schools. Children do not have proper provision to sit. They sit on the floor.

Table 7.17: School Type *vs.* Adequate Furniture

District	*Very Poor (%)*	*Poor (%)*	*Average (%)*	*Good (%)*	*Excellent (%)*
Government	76.47	15.68	3.92	1.96	1.96
Private	100.0	–	–	–	–
Total	**80.64**	**12.90**	**3.22**	**1.62**	**1.62**

Some of the Government and private schools in urban and rural areas are furnished poorly and very poorly.

Separate Toilets

Table 7.18: District-wise Separate Toilets for Girls and Boys

District	*No (%)*	*Yes (%)*
Ranga Reddy	36.36	63.63
Hyderabad	10.00	90.00
Medak	40.00	60.00
Nalgonda	18.18	81.81
MBNR	13.33	86.66
Total	**24.20**	**75.80**

Most of the schools (75.8%) have separate toilets for girls and boys.

Table 7.19: School Type *vs.* Separate Toilets for Girls and Boys

School type	*No (%)*	*Yes (%)*
Government	25.49	74.50
Private	18.18	81.81
Total	**24.2**	**75.8**

Table 7.20: Locality *vs.* Separate Toilets for Girls and Boys

Locality	*No (%)*	*Yes (%)*
Urban	14.28	85.71
Rural	27.08	72.91
Total	**24.2**	**75.8**

Most of the Government and private schools in urban and rural areas have separate toilets.

Table 7.21: District-wise Availability of Scavenger

District	*No (%)*	*Yes (%)*
Ranga Reddy	81.81	18.18
Hyderabad	40.0	60.0
Medak	73.33	26.66
Nalgonda	81.81	18.18
MBNR	86.66	13.33
Total	**74.2**	**25.8**

There are no scavengers available in the schools. Children clean their toilets on their own. It is very harnessing to continue with these sanitary conditions, where children and teachers do not have the minimum basic sanitary needs fulfilled. How can they be child-friendly?

Running water in Toilets: In almost all the districts, more than half of the schools (56%) do not have running water in the toilets. Most of the school toilets (70.9%) are not cleaned regularly. Most of the Government schools in rural areas do not have running water in their toilets. Also they don't have mugs and buckets and no running water. How can any toilet be functional?

In some schools, classrooms are not maintained properly. When they were asked why, they responded that there is no attender/*aaya,* so children in turns clean and keep the classrooms neat. It was also noted in many schools by the investigator when he visited the schools. In very few schools (20%) scavengers and *ayaas* are available. It clearly indicates that schools do not give any healthy and hygienic environment for proper growth and development of children which is in a way not protecting child rights i.e. violation of the rights.

Table 7.22: District-wise Drinking Water

District	*No (%)*	*Yes (%)*
Ranga Reddy	18.18	81.81
Hyderabad	0	100.0
Medak	20	80.0
Nalgonda	18.18	81.81
MBNR	80	20.0
Total	**30.6**	**69.4**

About 70 per cent schools have drinking water. The surroundings are not kept clean (40%) and also the water containing tanks are not cleaned regularly (40%). Teachers do report about the facilities in schools like water, toilets, scavengers and ayayas to the authorities (70%). However, there is no serious reciprocation or reaction or response from the authorities and at times teachers those who bring up the issues, are penalized for the same.

Table 7.23: District-wise Health Camps

District	*No (%)*	*Yes (%)*
Ranga Reddy	63.63	36.36
Hyderabad	90.0	10.0
Medak	80.0	20.0
Nalgonda	45.45	54.54
MBNR	80.0	20.0
Total	**72.6**	**27.4**

Health Camps: Most of the schools (72.6%) do not conduct health camps at regular intervals.

Table 7.24: District-wise Children with Neat Uniforms

District	*No (%)*	*Yes (%)*
Ranga Reddy	–	100.0
Hyderabad	–	100.0
Medak	20.0	80.0
Nalgonda	9.09	90.90
MBNR	80.0	20.0
Total	**25.8**	**74.2**

Most of the children (74.2%) come to school in neat uniform, however, in some rural schools (56%) they are not so neatly dressed.

Mid-day Meals: Most of the children (65%) do not eat mid-day meals. However, some children feel that food is not nutritious and provide routine meal regularly which includes dal and rice and children cannot relish it every day.

How Far Schools Equipped with Teaching Learning Material (TLM)

Table 7.25: District-wise Laboratory with Equipment/Chemicals

District	*No (%)*	*Yes (%)*
Ranga Reddy	18.18	81.81
Hyderabad	30	70
Medak	100	–
Nalgonda	18.18	81.81
Mahaboobnagar	60	40
Total	**50**	**50**

Laboratory: About 50 per cent of the schools have laboratory and sports material available. They even keep some recreating material for them too.

More than half (51%) of schools do not provide recreation and literary activities to students.

Table 7.26: District-wise Teaching Learning Material (TLM) Available

District	*No (%)*	*Yes (%)*
Ranga Reddy	45.45	54.54
Hyderabad	20	80
Medak	100	0
Nalgonda	27.27	72.72
Mahaboobnagar	66.66	33.33
Total	**56.5**	**43.5**

Teaching and Learning Material: Only 43.5 per cent of schools have TLM's adequately available in the schools and have displayed.

Books available to read: More than half of the schools have some books for children to read.

How far child rights practices are observed in schools?

Most of the teachers (69.4%) do not appreciate children in different situations, but they (54.8%) appreciate bright children. Majority (91.8%) of the teachers without being conscious, humiliate children who are slow learners by using discouraging words. Teachers (93.5%) neglect and do not pay much attention to slow learners.

It is observed that more than half of the teachers (56.5%) do not discriminate children with category of the children. They are all treated almost equally. Most of the time teachers (96.8%) focus specially on bright children. More than half of the teachers (58.1%) motivate/encourage boys and girls equally. However, in some schools mostly boys are encouraged whereas in other schools girls are encouraged more.

Teachers (58.1%) are patient and show tolerance towards children in various contexts, teachers (61.3%) treat children with care and affection. More than half of the teachers (62%) show anger and are harsh with children and give corporal punishment to children in the classroom. Teachers (62%) use abusive words towards children. Some teachers (38.7%) appreciate slow learners. Teachers (91.8%) do not treat properly the aggressive and mischievous children. Teachers (66.1%) do not treat different categories of children equally and discriminate (87.1%) children with community background. Teachers encourage (59.7%) children from different caste/creed and languages.

Teachers (59.7%) guide children with health problems and give direction to attend to health problems. Teachers (58.1%) inform parents on child's performance.

Teachers (59.9%) motivate parents to send children regularly to school. Some teachers (32.3%) also help children in learning difficulties, health problems (38.7%) higher studies and career guidance (32.3%), support family (45.2%), counseling (45.2%),. Some teachers (38.7%) also extend financial help to children in some contexts.

Based on the Classroom Observations How Far the Teacher Practices are Child Friendly?

Table 7.27: Based on the Classroom Observations of the Teacher Practices

More child-friendly (%)	*Less child-friendly (%)*
48.4%	51.6%

Teachers show concern and care towards the children, treatment of children in classroom while teaching, interaction with children and parents. How teachers help children to learn through motivation, appreciation, guidance and so on.

Based on observations, holistically the teacher's practices in the schools are reflecting their being child-friendly i.e., more child friendly (48.4%) and less child friendly (51.6%).

Table 7.28: District-wise Child-Friendly Schools

Sl. No.	*Districts*	*No. of Schools*	*No. of Schools Less Child friendly*	*No. of Schools More Child friendly*
1.	Ranga Reddy	10	90%	10%
2.	Hyderabad	10	80%	20%
3.	Medak	13	0%	100 %
4.	Nalgonda	10	100%	0%
5.	Mahaboobnagar	10	70%	30%

When observed in five districts particularly Medak district was found to be highly child-friendly 13 (100%). It is very encouraging and happy to note that there are no schools which are less child-friendly in Medak. On contrary, the schools which were observed in Nalgonda are all less child-friendly 10 (100%), where as in Ranga Reddy district nine (90%), Hyderabad eight (80%), Mahaboobnagar seven (70%) schools are less child-friendly. Holistically based on observation it can be stated that most of the schools except Medak are less child-friendly.

How far the Classroom Practices and Curriculum Transaction is Child-friendly?

More than half of the schools (56.5%) have pleasant, positive environment which promotes learning. Only in few schools (11.3%) teachers teach with planning according to the level of the child. Some places, more than half of the schools, teachers (51.6%) teach concepts very clearly.

On the day the observation was made, only few school teachers (25.8%) taught the lessons with good examples related to day to day living. Teachers (53.2%) could teach as per the interest of the children. It was even observed that (58.1%) teachers pay attention to all the children equally. More than half of school teachers (58.7%) exhibited care and concern for children in the class, also teachers (54.8%) encourage all categories of children. Teachers (58.1%) seem to be hard working to make children to excel. They are keen in terms of children's interests by monitoring keenly, teachers (59.7%) provide opportunity to express their feeling and opinions. Teachers (58.1%) motivate all children to learn and also respects (53.2%) child's interests, teachers (54.8%) also respects children. Only a little more than half schools (56.1%) are observed with active child-child interaction regularly.

Table 7.29: Child to Child Interaction

Interaction	*Per cent*
Never	16.1
Now and Then	40.3
Continuous	43.5
Total	**100.0**

Table 7.30: Child to Teacher Interaction

Interaction	*Per cent*
Never	41.9
Now and Then	16.1
Continuous	41.9
Total	**100.0**

Almost similarly the interaction between child-teacher is also observed.

Table 7.31: Child to Teaching Learning Material

Interaction	*Per cent*
Never	14.5
Now and Then	37.1
Continuous	48.4
Total	**100.0**

In a similar way it was observed the interaction between the child and teaching learning material.

This interaction shows that slightly more than half of the schools encourage child-centric practices and active participation of children and freedom to express their opinion.

How is Discipline Maintained?

Table 7.32: District-wise Disciplinary Practices

District	*More Child Friendly Practices*	*Less Child Friendly Practices*
Ranga Reddy	9.09	90.90
Hyderabad	10.0	90.0
Medak	100.0	–
Nalgonda	–	100.0
MBNR	80.0	20.0
Total	**40.3**	**59.7**

Some teachers (40.3%) treat children well, however, more than half of the teachers (59.7%) do not treat children well.

On the Whole How are Schools Doing with Classroom Practices? Are They Child Friendly?

Across five districts under study show that most of the (60.6%) schools look less child-friendly. Majority of them except Medak (100%), Mahaboobnagar (65.66%) are more child-friendly remaining three districts schools Ranga Reddy (100%), Hyderabad (100%), and Nalgonda (100%) are less child friendly.

Table 7.33: District-wise Child-Friendly Schools

District	*More Child friendly*	*Less Child friendly*
Ranga Reddy	–	100.0
Hyderabad	–	100.0
Medak	100.0	–
Nalgonda	–	100.0
Mahaboobnagar	66.6	33.33
Total	**40.32**	**59.67**

Also it is observed that most of the urban schools teachers (85.7%) practices are less child-friendly. It is very obvious that relatively number of schools under both Government and private managements are less child-friendly (60.6%) compared to schools which are more child-friendly (39.4%). From the investigators observations it is observed most of the schools are less child friendly. However, from children's perceptions and teachers self projections it appears to be more child friendly.

Chapter 8

Module on Child Rights for Training Teachers

Create Awareness on CRC

3D-Presentation for Training Teachers to Create Awareness on CRC

A presentation is prepared to create awareness on child rights and to develop sensitivity towards children's issues (*see* Annexure on pp. 133-134).

Module Consists of Three Dimensions

1. A presentation with children's pictures under different circumstances. Brief information on Child Rights is provided through slide presentation. (3D-presentation).
2. Teachers are made to enact short skits (one/two skits) reflecting their regular classroom attitude towards children.
3. Brochure giving list of rights with pictorial/symbolic representation, leaflet and posture

After designing the module it was tried out to establish validity and reliability.

Sequence of the Module during Training in Five Districts of Andhra Pradesh

1. First questionnaire consists of ten questions is given to teachers (Pre-test).
2. 3D-Presentation is shown.
3. Teachers are made to enact short skits.
4. Child Rights handouts—brochure, poster and leaflet are given (see

Annexures on pp. 144-150; *Source:* UNICEF). Teachers are made to read by giving 15 minutes time before they participate in the quiz.
5. Quiz consists of ten questions (Post-test).

Teachers are made to Enact Short Skits

1. A Classroom Scene

Teacher entres the classroom and start discussion with students.

Student asks teacher: When do we have winter holidays?

Teacher: You fool! You are always interested in holidays. You never show any interest in studies. Sit down.

Student becomes very depressed and lost all the enthusiasm. He silently weeps and sits at the back in the classroom after being hurt by teacher's words and remain silent for the whole day.

All his classmates giggle and make fun of him.

2. How should Teachers Respond?

Teacher entres into the classroom and observes for a while silently then:

Teacher: Why is the classroom very dirty and shabby? Why all the furniture is lying here and there. Do you keep your house like this? Come on girls, go and get a broom sticks and clean the classroom. Boys come and put all the furniture in order. I will get back to the class once you finish your work.

All students keeps quiet and looks dismayed and feels sorry for the teacher's reaction.

3. Children Playing in the Playground—Is it Crime to Play?

Principal goes for school round, suddenly finds group of children playing in the playground. He calls all the children and enquires, "Don't you have any classes? Why are you playing at this hour in the ground?

Students: We have free class, Sir!

Principal: Can't you sit in the library and read. You are playing like donkeys and wasting your time. You will never change. Get back to your classroom. Call your class teacher.

4. Do Teachers Listen to the Voice of the Students?

Class has already begun; a student walks into the classroom with his face down he feels shy because he is late to the class and dressed untidy.

Teacher: You are not dressed neatly. Is this the way you come to school?

Student tries to give the reason for his untidy dressing.

Teacher ignores, do not listen to the student's reply neither understand his feelings. Teacher makes the student stand in front of his classmates and continue to insult for his untidy dressing and all his classmates started laughing.

Student was humiliated before his classmates and afraid to talk about what happened in the school at home and he hates to come to school and decided to stay at home.

5. A Child can be Shaped from Praise/Encouragement, not by Punishment

Teacher asks all the students to keep quiet and not to make noise as principal will come for school round.

Student does not listen to what teacher says and still misbehaves and disturbs the whole class.

The teacher warns the student for his misbehaviour.

As principal entres the class and observes that the student is disturbing the whole class and then scolds the teacher before the students and leave the classroom.

Teacher gets very angry as principal scolded him before the students. He pulled the boy out and slapped him and holds his ears and lift the student up with his feet off the ground, and his ear twisted out of shape, the student cry out in pain with his mouth open.

His classmates feel pity for what had happened in the classroom and they are very frightened and express fear when they look at the teacher.

Pre-and Post-test Questions

1. In which year UN General Assembly adopted the Declaration of the "Rights of the Child"?
2. In which year the Government of India adopted the CRC?
3. Which countries have not ratified the CRC?
4. How many articles are there in the CRC charter?
5. How many parts/divisions are there in CRC?
6. How many categories of child rights are there?
7. Which articles are pertaining to education in CRC is similar to the Article 45 of Indian Constitution?
8. Who is considered as child in CRC?
9. Which age group children are considered as child labour?
10. Who should inform (and are responsible) the children about their rights?

Impact of the Module–Results–Discussion

Some of the sample schools were selected for training teachers to create awareness on child rights. First the principal investigator trained teachers at Hyderabad in one of the schools. During training the field assistants were made to observe and repeat similarly at the other schools in other districts.

As per the schedule planned, training was done. The scores of the performance of the teachers before and after the training was collected, analysed and are shown in the Table 8.1.

Table 8.1: Pre-and Post-test Results

Sl. No.	*Districts*	*Teachers*	*Mean*		*SD*		*t*
			Pre-test	*Post-test*	*Pre-test*	*Post-test*	
1.	Hyderabad	25	2	8	1.2	2.66	21.4
2.	Ranga Reddy	25	2	8	1.16	2.2	21.4
3.	Mahaboobnagar	20	1	6	0.89	1.2	19.35
4.	Medak	20	2	7	1.18	1.51	12.90
5.	Nalgonda	20	1	7	0.83	1.48	19.37

From the pre-and Post-test results it is observed that the mean score in the pre-test in all the groups is found to be very less i.e. the awareness on CRC is very poor. Also it is observed in the post-test the mean values are high which shows the awareness is increased when compared to pre-test.

The mean value is very low i.e. between 1-2 in the pre-test whereas in the post-test the mean values are high which shows that module impacted in developing awareness. Mean difference between pre-test and post-test is being high (Hyderabad 6, Ranga Reddy 6, Nalgonda 6, Mahaboobnagar and Madak 5 each). It can be stated that there is an impact of the module which must have created awareness in teachers. Further the difference between pre-test and post-test also found to be significant (probability value being below 0.005), it can be stated that the module is effective in developing awareness amongst the teachers.

Thus, it can be concluded that there is a positive impact of the module on the teachers in developing awareness on CRC. Almost all the districts showed a significant difference between pre-and post-tests and also it is found statistically significant.

In all the five districts teachers who are exposed to the module with the sequence mentioned gave a good results where teachers were found to be very enthusiastic and active while enacting the skits and also playing quiz which created a lot of interest in teachers. A small prize was also given to the winner group and a compliment to the loser group. Teachers also said in the informal discussion that they were not conscious that such small words would humiliate children. Likewise, teachers reflected very positively and also said they will be careful hereafter while dealing with children.

Real Life Stories of Children Reflecting Hidden Realities

1. Why 1000 Children Voices are not Heard?

No Freedom!

Sai Teja from a middle class background studies in a private Digi school. When the child was asked to write about his school and teachers, he gave a very gloomy picture where everything appears child friendly.

The child lives in a nuclear family along with his father, mother and elder sister. Child is pampered by the parents and is nurtured with full freedom.

His school is two storied big building with playground, aerated and ventilated (except two rooms). The school has 50 classrooms, 50 teachers, 1000 children, five smart boards, computer lab and science lab. Children play sports once in a week. When the child was asked to write everything, what he wrote was good. But in informal talks, child says, "Whatever my school brochure writes, half of it is not functional. We have smart boards but nobody use them regularly, science lab is there but not in use, only once in a week sports period is there.

Teachers do not teach well but ask children to read and memorise otherwise teachers beat them, scold them. Children should not speak/ask questions or complain to authorities (correspondent who comes on alternate days) or parents. If they complain, then those children are punished, humiliated in the classroom and are warned not to do so." Child feels that teachers do not give any extra information, day-to-day examples, etc. while teaching. All the children are scarcd of teachers and they don't like teachers. Only one or two teachers like Biology and Mathematics teachers teach well from textbooks (not encourage workbook alone). But they also beat if children do not study or make noise or do any small mistake. Almost all the teachers keep scolding children and come with a cane to classroom.

Child also says that the study hour after school 3-6 p.m. is just a waste; no child is interested to sit and memorise, no teacher teaches or cares about what children do. School also collects Rs. 500 per term for Vedic Maths. It is mandatory that every child has to pay though nothing is taught only books are given. Principle says, "We have paid in lakhs to them so you have to pay." Child says, "We don't like to be in school till 6 pm. Our teachers should not punish, speak well to children and teach well with day to day examples and use labs and smart boards".

Thus, school children are not happy with the school and teacher practices. But they have no freedom to express to parents or authorities. 1000 children are suffering and nobody to hear their voices.

2. Child Never Dares to say. Has no Idea as to what to do?

Helpless!

Twelve years old Kavya studying in a private school in VIth standard belongs to low socio-economic background. Father is a carpenter and alcoholic and mother is a housewife. This school is two floor building with 40 classrooms and an open ground to play and is up to Xth standard with round-about 800-900 school strength. Most of the private schools function on similar lines where they retain back the children in school in the name of study after school hours which frustrate the children.

When enquired about the school she told that her school is good and teachers are good. She says there is no games period, only when some teachers do not turn-up they are made to play in the ground. There is no library, no lab and no sports. Only at the time of annual day celebrations cultural activities take place. In everyday assembly, the group representatives conduct activities and some popular children are made to present news, quotations and general knowledge questions.

Children have no freedom. Just to follow whatever teacher says. This child says, we get tired by evening 6.30 p.m. The school is also far and at isolated place. Only two teachers really take care but other teachers just keep busy to themselves and ask children to sit and read of their own. Neither parents nor students say anything. Children do not even know how to express. Child says we have only two toilet in school and are not maintained neatly. When asked, "Don't you ask for more toilets?" She smiled and said how can we ask? No child is encouraged to ask or no child voice is heard in the school. It is all a game of strict rules, harsh punishment, scolding and punishments to children for any kind of deviations.

Children and parents just obey whatever schools say and give to children. Child feels that they should be free at least by 4.30 or 5.00 p.m. to relax and play. Children live in fear for the whole day from morning 9.00 a.m. to 6.30 p.m., with two short breaks.

Nutrition deficiency, no physical exercise, no proper rest, lot of emotional stress and mental pressure on children, and to add further that there is no freedom of expression. Is it not extreme violation of children rights?

3. Is it Right on Part of Teachers to Violate the Child Rights?

Exploitation!

A child Rukiya from a poverty stricken family was a puzzle for teachers when came to VIth standard after primary school. Child is very intelligent, smart, responds quickly from back bench to all questions posed by teachers. Teachers repeatedly call her to sit in the front. But the child lives in her own world and prefers to sit in the last bench.

One day all teachers pooled some money and brought clothes and distributed among the poor school children during Ramzan month. This child unconsciously spoke to a teacher that you are so nice. You are giving money for the poor children from your pocket. But my teacher at primary school made me to do all the domestic work and paid my mother only Rs. 500 as wage for three months. I used to go late to school, sit at the back and did whatever teachers say.

This story gives an astonishing ground reality about the teachers who are supposed to protect the rights are encouraging children to work at their home. Children are treated as slaves with disrespect and without any concern; and teachers are apathetic to children. Right to education is violated. Teacher made the child of 10 years as domestic worker and negotiates to work against Child Labour Act and violate the rights of the child.

Who should punish such teacher? How can the teacher violate the children rights?

4. Fate of Children in the Heart of the City. Why?

A child from a very poor socio-economic background stays in urban slum. She studies in Government school, goes regularly to school and she is very bright in studies. She has lot of interest in studies and wants to pursue higher studies. She has an aunt, father and mother at home.

Her hut is located just beside the *Nala* where dirty water almost flows through her house. The family was exposed to dirty water, germs and other infections. Her father, aunt and girl herself were got affected with infection and TB. Few months later all the three of them, one after the other died. Teacher narrated and felt sad about it when asked for any special issues on children in the school.

Where is the protection for children? Why is the right to life and health violated? Who is responsible?

5. Child Waits for Freedom of Expression!!

A boy studying in a private digi school in IXth standard belongs to middle class. He lives with his father, mother and brother. Though his father earns less as a private employee, yet sends both of his sons to a private school. He pays Rs. 500 per month for each child as school fee.

The boy says that all school teachers teach well but they do not have English teacher for about six months but no student or parents questions the authorities. They complete IXth standard syllabus by November or December and then they begin SSC syllabus from that time. They insist children to come to school during summer vacation. HM (Head Master) is very authoritative and very insensitive to children. Without any reason HM beats up children black and blue. But no parent comes to school to ask or complain. They think the HM is good and working for the good of children. All the children are scared and live in fear throughout the day in the school. There is no space for children to express themselves either in scholastic or non-scholastic aspects.

6. Child Goes to School Without Fear

A migrant hut dweller Shankuntala studies in a Government ZPHS school, 2-3 kms distance from her house. She goes to school in a bus sometimes she walks down to school, it takes 15 minutes.

Her family lives in a hut with three girls and two boys. One brother got married and has a child. One sister got married and has two children. Mother is daily wage labour, father sells plastic items. Younger brother who is 18 years old is still studying in VIIIth standard. As he has a problem of delay in speech he joined very late along with his younger sister who also joined late by two years to school. She is 16 years old but still in VIIIth standard.

This child feels very happy about the school with a big play ground, more than 1000 students and all teachers are concerned about children. Teachers motivate children to come regularly to school after attending to their domestic work so that we have good future. She is very thrilled by touching computers now and then and doing paint brush in MS Office. We do not have Science lab but we play games in computers and listen to songs in computer. We play and enjoy in school.

We have separate toilets for girls and boys. But mostly boys go out of the compound. We have graveyard and market on either side of our school. Toilets are cleaned only once in a month. Mid-day meal provided to us is cooked very soft suitable to month's old babies. Yet at times we eat and sometimes we do not relish. Twice in a week i.e. on Mondays and Wednesdays, boiled eggs are given. Mid-day meal is not very tasty.

Teachers beat whenever we do some mischievous things. Our teachers never scare us. They encourage us in all aspects. We have no fear and have freedom to say whatever we want to say with our teachers. Our teachers educate and train us with good words, "If you study well you will be benefitted." I love to go to school.

7. Go with What is There!!!

A 14 year-old Anita, her father is an auto driver, mother works as domestic labour. She is the youngest in the family, has sister and brother older to her. Her brother is pursuing B. Tech., IIIrd year—and sister polytechnic, IInd year. The family belongs to lower middle class. Child is very responsible and speaks positive about school. She studies in St. Mark School. It has one main branch and a sub-branch—where the child studies—has about 600 students with 10 classes, 20 teachers, with three floored building. On the ground floor there is small garden and some place for an assembly. Boy's toilets, five in numbers are on ground floor and three girl's toilets on the first floor.

There are Chemistry (Science lab) and Computer labs. School has two smart boards which are used by teachers now and then. Teachers teach well but they punish by using abusive language and also beat children if they do not do homework or do not study well or do any mischievous deeds.

Children stay back from 3.30 pm–6.30 pm for study hours, but not much work is done by children in that period. Children do not like to stay back. They feel like going home. Their parents also do not understand. They feel happy that their children are studying well. They never question school practices or teaching. Children want their teachers should not beat and should teach well. They should have more play time and not so long study hours.

8. Bright Child Drop-Out from the School Just for Rs. 500

Shekeera is studying in IXth standard in Government school, Hyderabad. She hails from a very poor socio-economic background. The child stays with her grandmother as she has no parents. The child is very good at her academic and otherwise. Due to poverty when her grandmother fell sick and could not continue to work, the child is withdrawn from the school and put to work in a hospital for a payment of Rs. 500 per month. In spite of teacher's request, child did not report back to school. Teachers and school were ready to pay Rs. 500 from their personal money. Still the child's grandmother refused to send her back to school. The school teachers and HM are taking interest and further negotiations are still continuing.

Who should give back her Right to Education?

9. Story of Nisha—Urban Slum Dweller from Hyderabad

Why Children Dropout?

Nisha is 14 years old girl dropout of school before completing VIIIth standard. Her father is a vegetable vendor and illiterate. Her mother is a housewife, but also engages in floral arrangement and sells in nearby areas in the evening every day.

Since Nisha is the oldest of four children in the family, she helps her mother in floral arrangements, separating bad buds, and knitting garlands. Apart from this, Nisha also helps in household chores, washing dishes, cooking and taking care of her younger ones. Nisha was a bright and a hard working student during her schooling. Her mother's aspirations were that she should study and become a Nurse. Nisha's mother used to have high regards for Nurses as they wore neat white dresses and look very pretty and work in big hospitals with big doctors. But, the situations in her house including debts, poverty, drunkard father, younger sisters and brother, mother's ill health kept Nisha away from school, not attending classes continuously and unable to appear in the exams, forcing her to eventually dropout from the school. Mother wants her to study and child also wants to go to school, but she is forced to dropout due to family responsibilities.

Who are responsible for her status? Is it not violation of her right to play and education?

10. Story of Radhika—Inability to Bear Educational Expenses

Is it not Child Enforced to Share of Economic Burden?

A peek into the lifestyle of urban slum presents a contrasting picture. The children are exposed to vulnerabilities that eventually steal their childhood. Their plight often drives them to work as child labour to support their parents or be a helping hand to their parents in petty professions that they are engaged to like vegetable vendors, cobblers, petty shopkeepers, etc.

Radhika dropped out of private co-education schools, Hyderabad in the middle of Grade VII when she was 13 years old. She decided to drop out because her parents were not able to pay her school fees. She mentioned that she tried to go to school and also worked as a part time in a shop as parents could not afford her school expenses.

Moreover, it was tiring for her to work and study at the same time. She did not have time to study at home; therefore, she decided to leave school. But she plans to continue the studies through private mode.

Who will sustain the motivation of the child to go with private Education? Is it a nightmare in the context? This is what is happening in the heart of many urban pockets.

11. Is There Security for Girl Children? Lack of Safety for Girl Child (Insecurity)

Insecurity for girls becomes a major obstacle to continue their school education. Sheetal, a good looking girl, dropped out in Grade VII as she was teased by the boys on her way to school.

Sheetal who lives in urban slum had to walks about 15 minutes to reach school. Three boys were following and teasing her every day. She told her mother about it, and her parents also cautioned/warned the boys. After one week the same boys started following her in spite of their parents warming. On hearing this, her mother got frightened and did not allow her to continue in school; even though she was good at her studies both parents are willing to send her to school.

Who is accountable for this incident?

Is it not the parents, teachers and school management responsibility to put her back in school?

12. Is the Child Lured to Earn than Learn?

Ambika, staying at Seethaphalmandi basti did not want to continue her studies as her friends in the slum had already discontinued their studies and were either learning embroidery, stitching, working with the beautician as helper and some of them engage themselves in their parents' occupation like selling vegetable, flowers, fruits, etc. Ambika's parents are illiterates, but they wanted their daughter to study and get a good job. They got her admitted in the Government school but she stopped going to school after two months. She said that she did not like to go to school alone. She is green with envy as her friends are learning as well as earning. She plans to join a beautician course as she can work and earn.

Who will teach the child to be aware of distractions? Who is accountable for child's decision? Who will work and make sure that all children get their rights?

13. Children are Unsafe and are Treated as Machines to Mind Scores Only

A missionary so called reputed school, where an eight year old child studies in IIIrd standard. Very active, dynamic, frequently asks questions in the class and plays a very dynamic role during parent-teacher meetings, oral discussions and in playground. She is very quick in grasping and responding in the class. This child has a visual problem which was developed when she was 19 months old in simple incidence at home. Child has fallen down with small tea cup in her hand which broke as she fell and small trace of it pierced into her pupil of left eye. After a great effort and pain underwent by the child, it was located and removed with subsequent three operations. This created such a great loss for the child. She cannot visualised or write on par with her age children. This puts her last in writing reading, copying from the blackboard and is labeled as hopeless child by the teacher. Teachers do not allow her to go out in the break or allow her to take food instead that time is used to complete her work. Out rightly teachers humiliate, abuse, become angry and often complained to parents or principal.

Class teacher has gone to the extent of making it as a big issue by complaining it with the principal and openly humiliated before everybody at the principal office. That night child could not sleep became furious about everything that happened around her. Child became very fearful and dejected with such experiences. But still the child does not want to withdraw from the school as she loves her school and friends. She cannot imagine going to other school when her parents want to change the school. The child said, "Please I would like to continue in this school." The story is narrated by her parents and grandparents, the child asks repeatedly to her grandparents if they can do anything for her to overcome the problem?

Who were supposed to protect and take care of the child during the school hours, instead torment child? Why should an innocent child undergo such a trauma for no fault of her? Is it the place for such a child to cope? What kind of training is provided to the teachers and authorities (Principal) of that school? Is it not right to label the school as inhuman school? Are we not responsible for violation of Rights? How much is our contribution to combat? Let us all reflect, respond and act..........!!!

Chapter 9

Reflections, Concerns and Future

Significant Observations and Realities

It is very essential that human beings behave like human beings with feelings and concern for other fellow humans more so to children. Adults' world is responsible for protecting children's rights. It is the moral obligation on part of parents, teachers, community and state at large to give the due rights to children, bring them up as responsible future citizens at national as well as global level. Such a high ideal is addressed by CRC in various angles in the convention, but in reality what is captured from the field is not very convincing as some of the views given by the respondents (teachers, children) are for social acceptance. However, certain naked realities are encapsulated.

To review whether the objectives have been achieved and the hypotheses are realised a snapshot of findings with discussion presented to grapple the outcomes of the study.

Objective 1: To Know the Awareness Levels of Teachers on Child Rights

Hypothesis 1: There will be difference in the awareness levels of teachers on child rights.

Major Findings

1. Most of the teachers show low level of awareness on child rights convention (CRC).
2. There is a significant difference in the level of awareness of teachers on CRC.
3. There is a significant difference in the level of awareness in teachers on CRC with respect to gender.
4. There is a significant difference in the level of awareness in teachers on CRC with respect to type of school management.

5. There is no significant difference in the level of awareness in teachers on CRC with respect to qualification.

From the findings it is very obvious that objective one is achieved and the hypothesis 'one' is realised, except with respect to qualification.

Also from the observations and the informal discussions, teachers reveal that there are no training programmes or discussion related to children rights and they are not very clear about the convention and various inclusions and how to protect children's rights in their schools.

Nowhere was it focused in any training programmes about the strategies or approaches to protect children except for a ban on corporal punishments and some of the child centered methods of teaching. Probably, some teachers who were trained were also not in position to recollect specific inclusions and their implementation to the fullest extent. This gives a clear direction in spite of more than two decade of CRC's enactment no clear signals are seen in the direction of protecting child rights.

It is very disappointing to believe the results found from the study that most of the teachers have no awareness about child rights convention irrespective of their background (gender, type of school management, qualification, etc.). They are not familiar with the inclusions in the convention. No way has teachers showed any interest or have knowledge about the various aspects of CRC. Many have not even received training in this regard.

Objective 2: To Probe into Sensitivity of the Teachers on Issues Related to Children

Hypothesis 2: Teachers are not sensitive towards issues related to children

Major Findings

1. Most of the teachers are positive in physical dimensions related to treatment of children in the classroom.
2. Most of the teachers are sensitive in their curriculum transaction and communications with children in the psychological and emotional dimensions.
3. Most of the teachers do not exploit or harass children sexually.
4. Most of the teachers do not put any restriction on children related to social and cultural practices in the school.
5. Most of the teachers show concern towards children health related practices at school.
6. Most of the teachers take care of hygiene practices at school.

7. Most of the teachers show concern about the poor sanitary facilities at schools.
8. Most of the teachers are child friendly irrespective of their age, management, gender, qualification, locality, subject background, experience i.e. teachers are sensitive towards children's issues.
9. There is a significant difference in teacher's practices and their sensitivity towards children.

From the above findings it can be stated that the second objective is achieved and the second hypothesis is not realised i.e. from the finding it shows teachers are sensitive towards issues related to children.

From the results it is very clear that teachers show sensitivity in their practices. However, most of the studies, media and other agencies have focused the negative results related to children's issues and school practices. Only negligible percent of teachers show concern for the existing facilities at schools. They show their inability to report or rectify the problems in schools, as the authorities do not cooperate or give a positive hearing to teacher.

Objective 3: To Inquire into the Practices of Teachers in the Classrooms

Hypothesis 3: Teachers show child friendly practices in classrooms/schools

Major Findings

Based on teachers personal responses:

1. Most of the teachers encourage children in academics.
2. Most of the teachers motivate children to come regularly to school.
3. Most of the teachers encourage parents to send their children to school.
4. Most of the teachers use innovative methods in the classroom teaching.
5. Most of the teachers say children like play-way methods.
6. Most of the teachers conduct remedial classes.
7. Teachers show special interest in giving awareness to children from poor socio-economic background on governmental benefits.
8. Most of the teachers use positive disciplinary practices.

Based on the Checklist Findings–Investigators Gactual Reporting

1. Most of the schools are having child friendly practices in the classroom.
2. More than half of the schools have pleasant positive learning environment.

3. Children interest was sustained in the classroom.
4. Teachers also give day-to-day examples.
5. Teachers pay attention, treat equally all the children irrespective of their background.
6. Teachers encourage children to express their opinion.
7. There is a child to child interaction happening regularly in more than half of the schools.
8. About half of the schools regular teacher to child interaction is observed in the classroom.
9. In little less than half schools there is a regular interaction between children to teaching learning material.
10. Teachers do not adopt any harsh disciplinary practices in the classroom.

From the findings it is observed that the objective three (3) is achieved and the hypothesis three is realised.

From the observations and results that teachers are very friendly, good, caring. Probably the basic nature of a teacher is good, some of the good, committed teachers were reflected in the selected sample might have brought such results.

Many teachers were also very vocal and gave a number of suggestions to improve the functioning of schools and practices of teachers in making good citizens. Also teachers shared many of their best practices which they feel are yielding good results.

Objective 4: To Find Out the Perception of Children on Classroom Practices

Hypothesis 4: There will be difference in the perception of children on classroom practices.

Major Findings

1. Most of the children expressed that in physical facilities like furniture, spaces are adequate and teaching learning material is also good.
2. Most of the children opine that the school environment is maintained well and kept clean.
3. Most of the children are guided by the teachers in case of health problems and monitor them.
4. Most of the children felt that teachers are very child friendly in the classroom.
5. Teachers are caring and concerned about each and every child and do not discriminate any child.

6. Most of the children said that teachers pay attention to slow learners through remedial instruction.
7. Most of the children felt that the teachers are very cooperative with children and their staff members.
8. There is a significant difference in the children perception on classroom practices.

From the finding it is clear that the objective four has been achieved and the hypothesis four is realised.

From the result and informal discussion it is understandable that most of the children revealed hard realities unconsciously during informal talks where teachers punish, beat, scold, humiliate, use abusive words, etc.

Majority of positive views could be due to the fear of the teachers or may be giving responses which are socially acceptable and appreciated by the adult world. Also teachers could be good due to ban on corporal punishment or it could be due to governmental interventions being active. As children being innocent and sensitive and do not express themselves out of fear and hide themselves many facts and also reveal positively about everything unconsciously.

Objective 5: To Design a Module on Child Rights for Training Teachers to Create Awareness on CRC.

Hypothesis 5: Module will develop awareness in teachers on child rights.

There is a significant difference between level of awareness in teachers before and after exposure to the module.

From the findings it is clear that the objective five has been achieved and the hypothesis five is realised.

From the result and discussion with teachers it is easy to note that the module designed is based on the simple examples and day to day events. Some of the skits made the teachers to play their role unconsciously created a clear understanding on the meaning of children rights. The way the 3D presentation created a simple way of running through children under different circumstances and also certain important highlights of the convention were focused and reinforced into teachers mind. Then the theoretical part of the module in the form of handouts related to children rights which might have helped teachers to play quiz and made them to remember well the rights related information without much difficulty. Probably the way the module was oriented made the teachers to develop better understanding of CRC.

When informal discussions held and open ended questions were posed to teachers and children. Some of the sharings and responses would reinforce the earlier results and hidden field realities.

Child Friendly Practices by Teachers

The reflection on various classroom practices of teachers look very child friendly, however, teachers have no clarity about it.

Investigator noticed that children are happy while learning. They reveal that children like activities, love to take active participation. Children like innovative methods. Teachers take care of all categories of children. They pay special attention to slow learners.

In teacher's words their practices are mostly child friendly, they also go by positive ways of dealing with children. Somehow the implications can be drawn that teachers put the children in discipline and teachers are objects of fear among children. Also teachers are happy about the majority of the facilities provided in schools. However, between 30-50 per cent schools reflected with inadequate facilities.

Children's Perception on School Practices

Most of the children are positive and happy about various facilities available in school (physical amenities, teaching-learning, space, environment, etc.). They also express very well about teachers care, concern and dealing with children in school and their treatment towards children in various school contexts, encourage participation.

Children reveal in the private talk and unconsciously here and there about the behaviour of teachers being strict, very harsh, punish, beat, threaten, scold, abuse and ill-treat children by making them to sweep or up-keep the classroom. The children fear some teachers because they are serious with children and also beat them and they are not child-friendly in their behaviour or practices

Few Qualitative Findings from Children Point of View: Verbatim Reflected

- My painful experience is when my friend was punished badly by my teacher in the classroom.
- My teacher scolded me one day, I cannot forget it.
- I want my teachers to be friendly as well as strict in studies.
- I fear my sir because he is always very serious.
- I fear my sir, he teach the lesson very seriously and frequently beat us.
- I fear buchibabu sir why because he wants us to be silent in the classroom if we misbehave or do not answer the questions he will beat us.

- I want my teachers to be friendly with us and help us in all the activities.
- We don't want study hours after school i.e. 3-6 p.m. where we learn nothing. Teachers don't teach anything and we cannot complain authorities (correspondent) or parents because if teachers know they punish, humiliate and beat us.

Teacher's Treatment of the Children in the Schools: Different Dimension

1. Physical Dimension: Majority of the teachers treating children well without abusing, without causing any physical injury, not giving physical punishment or man handling children either in the classroom or outside. Very few cases were noticed here and there.

2. *Psychological and Emotional Dimensions:* Mostly, teachers do not interfere into the cultural dimensions related to child's privacy or restrict any kind of cultural practices on children. There is no social discrimination or gender discrimination in day to day teacher's practices in the schools. Very few teachers are still with conservative practices (while walking you should not raise/bend your head) restrict children especially girls while eating, sitting and conducting various activities–playing, etc.

> 'In one of the Government co-education school teachers made a decision along with HM that in view of the girls-boys' intimacy and certain other problems, they made separate sections for boys and girls and they were not allowed to go together on school premises. They feel it is right to avoid certain consequences which they might have encountered in the past.'

3. *Health*: In most of the schools health camps are conducted regularly. Teachers do pay attention to the children if they are sick or any other health related issues. Teachers also explain to children about the health measures in different contexts. Also many teachers have personal talk with parents and children. Few teachers said that there is no health facility within the reach in many rural areas.

4. Hygiene: This is very poor in many schools. Mostly school premises, classrooms premises and classrooms are not properly maintained. Sanitary facilities are poor in half of the schools. Even buckets, mugs, running water in toilets are not available. However teachers help children in maintaining personal hygiene.

Teachers shared that they make personal contribution and appoint ayas and scavengers to clean toilets and classrooms. In some schools children clean classrooms in turns.

5. Nutrition: To look physically children appear (75%) healthy. It may be because of the food provided at home. However, children feel the midday meal provided is not very tasty and is routine. On the whole schools appear mostly child friendly in their practices.

6. School Facilities: Very few schools are provided with excellent physical facilities. Especially sanitary, water facilities are poor in most of the schools in all the five districts.

Mostly girls have no separate toilets in rural and some in urban schools. Wherever present they are not maintained properly. Building space is also not adequate in majority of the schools. It is observed except those covered under new building provision. Mostly, planning did not consider much on aeration and ventilation. Building ambience also not properly maintained in majority of the schools. Provision to play is also encouraging in most of the schools.

Health camps are conducted at regular intervals, in majority of schools. Mostly, children do not relish mid-day meals. Teaching learning materials is adequate in most of the schools. Laboratory facilities are available in about half of the schools but are not utilised. However, they provide some sports and recreation material to children.

In some schools teachers do not appreciate all categories of children they pay attention to meritorious children. Very few teachers unconsciously, humiliate some children with discouraging words. Teachers are good and concerned about children. Mostly, teachers are child-friendly in their classroom practices and also the curriculum transaction is child-friendly. Relatively Medak and Mahaboobnagar are more child friendly compared to other three

Districts Ranga Reddy, Hyderabad and Nalgonda which are less child-friendly.

What should be Our Future Concerns to Make Schools

More Child-friendly?

The insights from the study and the varied finding from different viewpoints necessitates the future to be more conscious about children to create a child friendly ambience, schools, teachers and parents and the whole system as such.

1. Authorities

1. Authorities should empower teachers and children with child rights widely. The media posters and other means should be used to create awareness and practice every day. It is a legal obligation on the

governance to create a transparent monitoring and funding in order to provide the best facilities and school ambience to attract the children especially in Government schools.

2. It is very essential to create a wide awareness amongst the teachers on rights of children and their role in providing children their due rights.
3. Teachers should be sensitised through media and other effective modes to realise their disciplinary acts can either make or correct the child.
4. Best practices should be recognised and shared with everybody. At the same time any deviation needs a serious disciplinary action which comes in the way of children's rights.
5. It is not enough just give funding to create big structures for schools without creating any space for maintenance. Along with teachers' recruitment, secretarial assistance, cleanliness, maintenance, security (watchman), compound walls and gate should be strengthened to upkeep the school premises and create healthy, hygienic and happy schools with happy and healthy children without any fear.
6. Requirement in the toilets should never be compromised. Child friendly schools with better sanitary conditions can solve many other problems for which serious interventions are made otherwise.
7. Children's views should be taken carefully and necessary care should be extended. Especially separate toilets with running water and related items.
8. Proactive system should be encouraged; children's opinions should be taken very seriously through various means (suggestion boxes, external agencies, sudden inspections, community views).
9. Child friendly curriculum with child centred methods and ensure participatory, responsible learning in schools.

II. Teachers

1. Teachers should become more conscious while transacting curriculum and teaching children and caring children.
2. Child friendly methods of teaching and practices should be given to teachers and they need to be recognised by the authorities to motivate all the teachers with such practices.
3. Teachers should know where to relax and where to restrict children to modify the behaviour.
4. Teachers should treat children empathetically with love, concern, affection and morality.
5. Teachers should be assertive in creating adequate sanitary facilities

for them and children by representing to the concerned authorities. Bring to the notice of the village heads, community leaders and parents to get an immediate attention. If necessary may be brought to media.

III. Children

1. *Need for awareness:* Wide range of programmes, posters, curriculum should create awareness among children about their rights.
2. Various teaching-learning strategies should provide space for children's participation and reflections.
3. Children should be made as members in various committees and provide an opportunity to be decisive (children clubs, children forums, child panchayats, children as a part of various committees).
4. Mechanisms should be created to identify the violation of child rights in schools through simple feedback from children on school and teachers.
5. Children should be trained in both enjoying their rights and discharging their responsibilities by being empathetic to others rights.
6. Children panchayats and committees should be created and conducted regularly under the monitoring state committees/members in privacy to capture the realities.
7. Children made to participate in creating and displaying posters and captions related to child rights. Children should be given freedom to express anonymously about their feelings, emotions and opinions on the functioning, status and suggestions to improve their schools.
8. Children committees to monitor various facilities of the schools and reporting in their words to the community leaders, parents, authorities and media regularly.

Since today's child is tomorrows responsible citizen. It is very essential to take various angles and create sincere, committed and concerted efforts by every member of the society to create a world of happy, healthy children of today and a responsible productive citizen member of tomorrow.

References

Aiken, W. and LaFollette, H. (1980*). Who's Child? Parental Rights, Parental Authority and State Power,* Totowa, NJ: Rowman and Littlefield.

Alston, P. (1994). *The Best Interests of the Child: Reconciling Culture and Human Rights,* Oxford: Clarendon Press.

Archard, D. and Skivenes, M. (2009). "Balancing a Child's Best Interests and a Child's Views", *International Journal of Children's Rights*, 17: 1-21.

Archard, D. (1993). *Children: Rights and Childhood*, London: Routledge.

Acehnese teachers educated in child rights, www.alertnet.org

Anetta Tousheva, (2002). *Protecting Children's Rights in the Information Society* (http://cis-acp.government.bg) Backgrounder Child Labour in Agriculture Human Rights Watch Publication, ILO.

Barries, J.M. (1995). *Peter Pan and Other Plays,* edited with an Introduction by Peter Hollindale, Oxford: Oxford University Press.

Bellingham, John. (2002) *Dictionary of Education*, Academic India, New Delhi-110 008.

Benatar, D. (2008). *Better Never to Have Been*: *The Harm of Coming into Existence,* Oxford: Oxford University Press.

Brighouse, H. (2003). "How Need to Children be Heard?" *Arizona Law Review*, Fall: 691-711.

Buchanan, Allen E. and Brock, Dan W. (1998). *Deciding for Others: The Ethics of Surrogate Decision Making,* Cambridge: Cambridge University Press.

Child Welfare Scheme (2005), *Initiatives to Combat Child Abuse Research Report*, Child Welfare Scheme, Nepal.

Children and Youth in emerging and transforming societies www.childwoods2005.uio.no

Convention on the elimination of all forms of discrimination against women.

Covell and Howe, R.B. (1999). "The Impact if Children's Rights Education: A Canadian Study". International Journal of Children's Rights.

Covell, K. (2001). Children's Rights Education: A New Reality for Teachers Educator Canada.

Eekelaar, J. (1986). "The Emergence of Children's Rights", *Oxford Journal of Legal Studies, 6:161-182.*

Elster, J. (1989). *Solomonic Judgements, Studies in the Limitations of Rationality,* Cambridge: Cambridge University Press.

Farson, R. (1974). *Birthrights*, London: Collier Macmillan.

Feinberg, J. (1980). "A Child's Right to an Open Future", In: W. Aiken and *H. LaFollette, H., Whose Child? Parental Rights, Parental Authority and State Power,* Totowa, NJ: Littlefield, Adams, and Co: 124-153.

Griffin, J. (2002). "Do Children Have Rights?", In: *The Moral and Political Status of Children:* New Essays, D. Archard NAD c. Macleod (eds.), Oxford: Oxford University Press: 19-30.

Gender and Education for all: The leap to Equality, Summary report, UNESCO, Paris. www.unesco.org/education/efa report/summary en.pdf.

Government of India (2003*) Education for all: National Plan of Action.*

Hart, H.L.A. (1973). "Bentham on Legal Rights", In: A.W. Simpson (ed.). *Oxford Essays in Jurisprudence,* 2nd series, Oxford: Clarendon Press: 171-201.

Haq. (2005). *Centre for Child Rights. Status of Children in India Inc.*

Holt, *J.C. (1975). Escape from Childhood: The Needs and Rights of Children,* Harmondsworth: Penguin.

Human rights watch (2001). *Scared at school: Sexual violence against girls in South African Schools*, Human Rights Watch, New York.

Importance of revamping the University curriculum www.yementimes.com

Increased awareness of Child Rights creates positive change http://www.lu.se.

Increasing Awareness on CRC in Schools and Communities http://www.unicef.org.

International Labour Organization (ILO) (2005). *A global alliance against forced labour, ILO, Geneva.*

Juneja, Nalini (2005). *The Primary Teacher (The rights of children in school to be free from fear),* NCERT, New Delhi.

Kopelman, L.M. (1997a). "Children and Bioethics: Uses and Abuses of the Best-Interests Standard", *The Journal of Medicine and Philosophy* 22:213-17

Kopelman, L.M. (1997b). "The Best-Interests Standard as threshold, Ideal, and Standard of Reasonableness", *The Journal of Medicine and Philosophy*, 22:271-289.

Kramer, M.H. Simmonds, N.E. and Steiner, H. (1998). *A Debate Over Rights, Philosophical Enquiries,* Oxford: Clarendon Press.

Kothari, C.R. (2002), *Research Methodology*, New Age International (P) Ltd., New Delhi.

LeBlanc, Lawrenece J. (1995). *The Convention on the Rights of the Child. United Nations Lawmaking on Human Rights*, Lincoln; University of Nebraska Press.

Liao, S.M. (2006). "The Right of Children to be Loved", *The Journal of Political Philosophy*, 14(4): 420-440.

MacCormick, N. (1982). Children's Rights: A Test-Case, in his *Legal Right and Social Democracy*, Oxford: Clarendon Press: 154-166.

McGough, Lucy S. (1995). "Children: V Child Custody", In: W.T. Reich, Editor in *Chief Encyclopedia of Bioethics*, Revised edition, New York: Simon and Schuster Macmillan: 371-8.

Mills, Claudia. (2003), "The Child's Right to an Open Future?" *Journal of Social Philosophy*, 34(4) *Winter*: 499-509.

Mnookin, Robert H. (1979). "Foster Care—In Whose Best Interests?" In: O'Neill, O. and Ruddick. W. (eds.) *Having Children: Philosophical and Legal Reflections on Parenthood,* Oxford: Oxford University Press: 179-213.

Master of Advanced study's in children's Rights 2007-08 (2006), (http://www.iukb.ch/mcr)

Millions of children still not in school, http://www.unicef.org

Juneja, Nalini (2005). *The Primary Teacher (The rights of children in school to be free from fear)*, NCERT, New Delhi.

Narendra Reddy. C (2003). *Human right education must for a developing Society*, Recent Researches in education and Psychology, Mrs. Asha Gupta, Chandigarh.

O'Neill.O. (1988). *Children's Right and Children's Lives, Ethics*, 98:445-463.

Purdy, L.M. (1992). In Their Best Interest? The Case against Equal Rights for Children, Ithaca and London: Cornell University Press.

Wazir, Rekha (2002). *Getting out work and into school monograph,* M.V. Foundation, Hyderabad.

Rights and Equiry in the Classroom, www.unicef.org/evaldatabase/index.html

Rawls, J. (1999). *A Theory of Justice*, Revised Edition, Oxford: Oxford University Press.

Sandel, M. (1982). *Liberalism and the Limits of Justice*, Cambridge: Cambridge University Press.

Scarre, G. (ed.). (1989). *Children, Parents, and Politics*, Cambridge: Cambridge University Press.

Schoeman, F. (1980). "Rights of Families: Rights of Parents, and the Moral Basis of the Family", *Ethics*, 91: 6-19.

Summer, L.W. (1987). *The Moral Foundation of Rights*, Oxford: Clarendon Press.

School Orphanage in Shuvelan, http;//www.madad.net

Sharma, R.A. (2002) *Advanced Statistics in Education and Psychology,* Surya Publication.

Small Change (2002), Bonded Child Labour in India's Silk Industry.

Tainted Harvest: (2002) *Advanced Statistics in Education and Psychology*, Surya Publication.

Teacher's Awareness of child rights in Ghanaian Basic Schools—Unicef evaluation database.

The forgotten killer of children.http://www.unicef.org/publications//files/Pneumonia The Forgotten Killer of Children.pdf.

The Millennium Development Goal on child mortality. www.unicef.org

The Small Hands of Slavery bonded Child Labour in India (1996).

The state of the world's Children 2007 http://www.unicef.org/publications/files/The*State of the World's Children 2007e.pdf*

Turning a Blind Eye; Hazardous Child Labour in EI Salvador's Sugarcane Cultivation (2004)

UNICEF (2004). The State of the World's Children, UNICEF

United Nations Millennium declaration. United Nation's New York http://www/un.org/millenium/declaration/areas552e.htm&http://www.developmentgoals.org

Vikasana (2005). Child Labour Rehabilitation Center (Bridge School)

Wilbroad Ngambi, ANPPCAN Uganda Chapter, anppcan@infocom.co.ug

World Bank (2000). World Development Repot 2000/2001: Attacking Poverty, Washington: World Bank

Wald, M. (1979). *Children's Rights: A Framework for Analysis, University of California at* Davis Law Review 12(2):255-282

Worsfold, V.L. (1974). "A Philosophical Justification for Children's Rights", *Harvard Educational Review*, 44(1): 142-57.

1946-2006 *Sixty Years for Children*

http://www.hindu.com/2005/09/30/23hdline.htm

http://www.unicef.org/publications/files/Inspirational Women.pdf

http://www.unicef.org/publications/files/19462006 Sixty Years for Children.pdf

http://www.savethechildren.in/medianews/news-releases.html

http://www.crin.org

http://www.crin.org/docs/Annual report final final.pdf

Appendix–A

Questionnaire on Awareness of Teachers towards Child Rights

PART–A

Teacher Profile

1.	Teacher Name	:	
2.	Qualification	:	
3.	Teaching Subject	:	
4.	Age	:	
5.	Years of Teaching Experience	:	
6.	Gender	:	Male/Female
7.	Religion	:	
8.	Cast/Community	:	OC/BC/SC/ST
9.	School Name	:	
10.	School Name	:	Private/Govt./Aided/Others
11.	Locality	:	Rural/Urban

PART–B

Sl. No.	*Questions*	*Responses*
1.	Did you read the child rights convention?	
2.	Did you get any training on child rights?	
3.	In which year UN General Assembly adopted the Universal Declaration of Human Rights?	
4.	In which year UN General Assembly adopted the Declaration of the "Rights of the Child"?	
5.	In which year the Government of India adopted the CRC?	
6.	Which year is the international year of the child was sponsored by UN?	
7.	How many countries have ratified the convention on the	

Sl. No.	*Questions*	*Responses*
	Rights of the Child?	
8.	Which countries have ratified the CRC?	
9.	How many articles are there in the CRC charter?	
10.	How many parts/divisions are there in CRC charter?	
11.	How many parts/divisions are there in CRC charter?	
12.	How many articles are present in Part-I	
13.	How many articles are present in Part-II	
14.	How many articles are present in Part-III?	
15.	How many categories of rights are there in CRC?	
16.	Which article do you think deal with non-discrimination?	
17.	Article-3 deals with which category of child rights?	
18.	Article-6 deals with which category of child rights?	
19.	Article–12 emphasizes on which aspect of a child rights?	
20.	Which articles are pertaining to education?	
21.	Which articles have focused on child abuse?	
22.	Which articles recognize the child to be protected from economic exploitation?	
23.	Which article protects the child from all forms of sexual exploitation and sexual abuse?	
24.	Which article gives provision to the disabled children?	
25.	Which articles represent Right to Participation?	
26.	On what basis do you think children are discriminated in the class/school?	
27.	Which article in CRC is similar to the article–45 of Indian constitution?	
28.	Which articles is pertaining to violence?	
29.	At what age children are recruited to armed forces?	
30.	Which groups of children are considered as child labours?	
31.	Who should inform the children about their rights?	

PART-C

QUESTIONNAIRE ON PRACTICES OF TEACHERS IN THE CLASSROOMS

1. All categories of children join in your school (SC/ST/BC/OC) : Yes/No
2. I encourage children to come regularly to school? : Yes/No
3. Many children drop-out from your school? : Yes/No
4. I encourage children in academics and regular attendance to school? : Yes/No
5. Parents respond to us whenever we call them. : Yes/No
6. Generally students do not show any interest to come to school. : Yes/No
7. I motivate children to come to school regularly : Yes/No
8. I encourage parents to send their children to school. : Yes/No
9. I am regularly observant about children's problems : Yes/No
10. Parents and community oppose me if I give suggestions about their child : Yes/No
11. I give awareness to children from low socio-economic background about the benefits. : Yes/No
12. Children from low socio-economic backgrounds do not show interest in coming to school? : Yes/No
13. Regularity and punctuality of children helps in effective teaching. : Yes/No
14. Sometimes I get bored with the routine teaching. : Yes/No
15. Mostly I use lecture method to teach lessons. : Yes/No
16. It is difficult for me to use innovative methods in the classroom. : Yes/No
17. Most of the children like activity, play way, project methods. : Yes/No
18. I find very enriching experiences everyday in my class room. : Yes/No
19. We have adequate Tg-Lg material at school to teach effectively. : Yes/No
20. Authorities should give good Tg-Lg material/equipment. : Yes/No
21. Present school curriculum is interesting for teachers and students. : Yes/No
22. I cannot tolerate children with indiscipline. : Yes/No

23. Children should not be given extra freedom. : Yes/No
24. Parents should take interest in their children studies. : Yes/No
25. Our school conducts remedial and special classes for slow learners. : Yes/No

Tick marks ( ) the facilities you have adequately in you school.

- Teaching-Learning Material
- Physical facilities
- Classroom environment
- School premises
- Sanitary facilities
- Training to teachers
- Experiences to children
- Extra-curricular activities

26. We conduct formal/informal tests regularly. : Yes/No
27. We also use Portfolio assessment–CCE (continuous comprehensive evaluation)/Competency based Evaluation in the school. : Yes/No

Please write about the best practices of your school which you want to share with other teachers?

Appendix-B

Opinionnaire on Children Perceptions

PART-A
CHILD PROFILE

1. Child Name :
2. Class :
3. Gender : Mala/Female
4. Age/Date of Birth :
5. School :
6. Type of the Family : Joint Family/Nuclear Family/Federal Family
7. No. of Family Members :
8. Occupation of Father :
9. Occupation of Mother :
10. Qualification of Father :
11. Qualification of Mother :
12. Locality : Urban/Rural
13. District :

PART-B
SCHOOL FACILITIES

1. Classrooms are provided with adequate facilities. : Yes/No
   a) Furniture : Yes/No
   b) Teaching–Learning materials : Yes/No
   c) Space : Yes/No
2. School environment is always maintained well and surroundings are kept clean. : Yes/No
3. School provides safe drinking water facility to children. : Yes/No
4. Sanitary facilities are adequate for all the children in the school. : Yes/No
5. Sanitary facilities are maintained neatly in the school : Yes/No
6. Teachers monitor children's health problems/guide the children : Yes/No

7. School conducts health camps/checkups : Yes/No
8. Teachers are very friendly in the classroom/school : Yes/No
9. Teachers come to class very regularly : Yes/No
10. Teachers never absent themselves : Yes/No
11. Teachers treat all the children equally irrespective of their background : Yes/No
12. Teachers give opportunity to all the children in doing different tasks/activities : Yes/No
13. Teachers help out the slow learners and children from poor backgrounds : Yes/No
14. Teachers are caring/concerned about each and every child in the class. : Yes/No
15. Teachers teach the lessons clearly. : Yes/No
16. Teachers teach the lessons very interestingly. : Yes/No
17. Teachers teach lessons by using Audio-Visual material. : Yes/No
18. Children get lot of motivation from the teachers to come to school regularly : Yes/No
19. Teachers never abusive words/bad language with children : Yes/No
20. Teachers are favourable to some children. : Yes/No
21. Teachers like the children who are a) smart b) rich c) belongs to high caste and shows discrimination. : Yes/No
22. Some teachers punish the children very badly : Yes/No
23. Some teachers regularly beat up the children : Yes/No
24. Teachers are very cooperative with each other : Yes/No
25. Teachers are very cooperative with children : Yes/No
26. Teachers are very cooperative with parents. : Yes/No
27. Teachers are very cooperative with community : Yes/No
28. Teachers like children/help children when required : Yes/No
29. Which teacher you like the most and why? :

PART-C
PERCEPTION OF CHILDREN ABOUT TEACHERS AND THEIR TEACHING IN THE CLASSROOM

1. Do you like your teachers teaching in the classroom- Yes/No
   If Yes why? ....
   If No why? ....

2. Which teacher do you like the most and why?

   ....

3. Are you fearful of any teacher? If so why?

   ....

4. How do you want your teachers to be with you?

   ....

5. If you become a teacher what you want to do?

   ....

6. Give memorable experiences that you had in the class room/school

   ....

7. Give unforgettable, painful experiences that you had from class room/school

   ....

8. How do you want your teacher to teach you?

   ....

9. Do you understand what teachers teach you?

   ....

10. Does your teachers encourage asking questions?

    ....

Please write the narrative/Story on each of the question on functioning of your school based on the following questions:

11. What is the best in your school?
12. (a) What do you want to say about your school?
    (b) What do you want to say about your friends?
    (c) What do you want to say about your teacher?
    (d) What do you want to say about your parents?
13. What are the suggestions you give for your school with regard to:
    (a) School Environment
    (b) Physical Facilities
    (c) Tg-Lg Material
    (d) Children
14. How do you want your school to be loved by you?

Appendix-C

Investigator Observation Schedule

Please observe the teacher in the classroom and write the observation beside each item or put a tick () if observed.

1.	Teacher Name	:	
2.	Qualification	:	
3.	Teaching Subject	:	
4.	Age	:	
5.	Years of Teaching Experience	:	
6.	Gender	:	Male/Female
7.	Religion	:	
8.	Caste/Community	:	OC/BC/SC/ST
9.	School Name	:	
10.	School Type	:	Private/Govt./Aided/Others
11.	Locality	:	Rural/Urban

1. Physical

a) Hitting/beating with objects/cane
b) Physical injury of children by punishments
c) Giving physical punishments (standing on the desk/outside the classroom/in the class room/kneel down/beating on different body parts)
d) Man handling the children in different ways (mention if any)

2. Psychological/Emotional

a) Shaming children
b) Ridicule/use insulting words (mention any words used by teacher)
c) Creating fear through facial expressions/body language/frowning eyebrows/wide opening of eyes/tightening lips or mouth/shouting loudly/scolding with abusive words.
d) Threatening with consequences (for ex. If you don't do ___ will lead to _____)
e) Humiliating by manking them to do things which leads to shame/psychological distress/fear/pain

f) Isolating from others/group/from the class/school activities.
g) Being indifferent to child/children
h) Over dominating the child
i) Neglecting the child/not caring/not attending to their needs
j) III-treatment in the class/school/assembly
k) Children shows fear of teacher/fear of speaking
l) Not happy in the school/morrows/sorrowful

3. Sexual

a) Touching intimate/private organs purposely
b) Holding closely girl children (adolescent group) by male teacher
c) Having different looks/gazing at girl children.
d) Forcing to be with them after the class
e) Calling home for special tuitions
f) Pointing out on dress/other aspects of the child

4. Cultural/Social

a) Dress restriction on girls
b) Treating girl children with discrimination
c) Insisting on certain behaviour patterns
d) Telling girls to practice/to be with approved social norms
   - While eating
   - While playing
   - While talking to boys
   - While sitting
e) Refers to dominant caste groups practices as good and refers to lower communities/minorities groups as not etiquette/uncultured etc.
f) Teacher from upper casts insult children from low class by pin-pointing them
g) Finds fault with the language they use/always correct with dominant language.
h) Takes examples which are related to cultural practices
i) Specific habits, values, practices are insisted by the teachers to follow.

I. Hygiene

1. **Upkeep of the Classroom and School Ground/Premises**
   a) Availability of the dust bins in class room/school Yes/No

b) Dumping place for waste Yes/No
c) Regular disposal of waste Yes/No

2. Sanitary Facilities

a) Do they have adequate toilets? Yes/No
b) Do they have separate toilets for girls and boys? Yes/No
c) Is there sufficient water, buckets, and mugs available in the toilets? Yes/No
d) Do they have scavenging facilities? Yes/No
e) Are toilets cleaned regularly/maintained cleanly? Yes/No

3. Encourage children to wear clean and neat uniforms/ hygienic cloths? Yes/No

II. Health

1. Do teachers tell/talk to children about their health care? Yes/No
2. Is regular vaccination done for all children? Yes/No
3. At what intervals health checkups for the children are conducted in the school? Half-yearly/Annually
4. Is there primary health centre available in the village or nearby village? Yes/No
5. Is health worker available in primary health center? Yes/No
6. Teacher attending/caring children suffering from any health problems. Yes/No

III. Nutrition

1. Most of the children look healthy in thc school Yes/No
2. Teacher monitors mid-day meal distribution to children Yes/No
3. Teacher checks the quality of mid-day meal provided. Yes/No
4. Teacher promotes nutritional value in food. Yes/No
5. Teacher gives awareness on healthy practices/ nutritional diet. Yes/No
6. School maintains good/clean surrounding where the food is served. Yes/No

Any other information you would like to say, please write below:

....

....

Appendix-D

Child Friendly School Facilities Checklist

PART-A

School Name: ………………………………………………………………...

1. Physical Facilities

i. School Building Excellent/Good/Average/poor/very poor
ii. Building space
iii. Aeration
iv. Ventilation
v. Space in the classroom
vi. Building surrounding are clean/neat
vii. Playground Available
viii. Children allowed to play
ix. Furniture
x. Furniture suitable to child's needs (to the size of the child)
xi. Availability of dust bins/safe disposal of waste
xii. Separate toilets available for girls and boys

Gender	*Toilets are maintained neatly*	*Cleaned regularly*	*Running water available*	*Buckets/mugs available*
Girls				
Boys				

xiii. Classroom neatly maintained
xiv. Scavenger available
xv. Ayas available
xvi. Drinking water available
xvii. Drinking water–tank/pot/drum/any other
xviii. Drinking water surrounding area neatly kept
xix. Any other please write ……………………………………………
xx. If the facilities are not good school approaches authorities for better facilities in the school Yes/No
xxi. School conduct health camps/checkups Half-year/Annually
xii. All the children avail Mid-day meals.
xiii. Mid-day meal provided by the school is nutritious.
xiv. Children come to school with neat uniforms/clothes

II. Details/Particulars of School Children

xxv. Total of children in the school–Girls?
xxvi. Total of children in the school–Boys?
xxvii. No of children in the classroom–Boys?
xxviii. No of children in the classroom–Girls?
xxix. No of children from slums/poor socio-economic background
xxx. No of children other than regional language/local language
xxxi. No of children come from long distances (more than 1 KM radius)
xxxii. No of children come from long distance–mode of transport
xxxiii. No of children with special needs (ortho/any other
xxxiv. Total no of classes
xxxv. Total no of teachers
xxxvi. Tg-Lg (TLM) materials Adequate/Moderate/poor
xxxvii. Books to read Yes/No
xxxviii. Laboratory with equipment/chemical Yes/No
xxxix. Games/sports material Yes/No
xl. Recreation–literary activities Yes/No

PART-B
CLASSROOM OBSERVATION OR INFORMAL TALK WITH THE TEACHERS

Child Practices-Interaction (45 Minutes)

Classroom observation or can even collect through informal talk with the teachers.

Please tick mark () in the relevant column, If necessary

Always/Sometimes/Never

1. Teacher appreciates good looking children (as looking smart etc)
2. Teacher appreciates/show partiality to bright children
3. Teacher uses discouraging words/humiliates slow learners
4. Teacher neglects slow learners and do not pay attention.
5. Teacher encourages all categories of children equally. (Irrespective of their caste/creed/language)
6. Teacher focuses most of the time on bright children
7. Teacher encourages/motivates only boys.
8. Teacher encourages/motivates only girls.
9. Teacher encourages/motivates both boys and girls equally.
10. Teacher is patient and tolerant to children
11. Teacher treats children with affection and love.

12. Teacher shows anger/gives corporal punishment.
13. Teacher use abusive words to children
14. Teacher appreciates even slow learners
15. Teachers treat properly even aggressive/mischievous children
16. Teacher treats all categories of children equally
17. Teacher point out children with their community background
18. Teacher observes and notes the health conditions of children
19. Guides/helps children with health problems
20. Provide direction to attend health problems
21. Negotiates/informs to parents on child's performance
22. Motivates parents to sent the children regularly to school
23. Helps children in different contexts
    a) Learning difficulties
    b) Health problems
    c) Financial problems
    d) Facilities etc
    e) Higher studies/career guidance
    f) Family support
    g) Counseling
24. Provide facilities/support children financially/morally

PART-B & C
PRACTICES OF TEACHERS IN CLASSROOM DURING CURRICULUM TRANSACTION

Teachers Interaction with the Students in the Classroom

Yes/No

1. Teachers call children by name
2. Teachers use specific words/nicknames/terms to address some children
3. Teacher segregates girls and boys in the classroom
4. Teacher do not collaborate boys and girls in assigning tasks.

Classroom Environment

5. Positive classroom environment/pleasant environment for the students to learn
6. Teachers teach according to the level of children.
7. Teacher teaches all the concepts very clearly.
8. Tells good examples/relates teaching to everyday living.
9. Teach according to the interests of children

10. Attention is paid to all types of children equally
11. Care/concern for all categories of children.
12. Encourages all categories of children to learn
13. Works hard to excel every child
14. Monitor keenly the interest of children
15. Gives full freedom to express their feelings
16. Provide opportunity to express their opinions/feelings
17. Motivates all the children to learn
18. Respect the child's interest.
19. Appreciates the children.

Continuous/Now and then/Never

20. Child-child interaction
21. Child-teacher interaction
22. Child-Tg-Lg interaction

Discipline

23. Positive treatment of children Yes/No
24. Using appreciative words
25. Maintains perfect discipline/silence in the classroom
26. Children keep moving talking to other children frequently
27. Teacher goes around the classroom and monitors children individually
28. Threatens children/punish harshly
29. Uses unpalatable language
30. Asks children to express their opinion on all aspects
31. Teachers consciously make every child to speak and also take part actively
32. Teachers show concern for children.

Annexures

Newspaper Stories

No proper accommodation in government schools

Child marriage averted

Film on girl child rights screened

REGION 7

Student hospitalised after 'corporal punishment'

EDUCATION QUOTA

Poor kids suffer due to AP 'fund crunch'

12 KIDS FALL ILL AFTER STALE LUNCH

237 CORPORAL PUNISHMENT CASES FILED THIS YEAR

3 YEARS IN JAIL FOR CORPORAL PUNISHMENT

EDUCATION DRIVE

State to identify school dropouts

Over 80,000 children born with genetic disorders each year in State

Move to hold school entrance test against RTE Act

Child marriage averted

TRAGIC END

Dewormer chokes girl to death

School: Kushbu had problem breathing

School teacher, sarpanch transform village

BOY TOLD TO DO 50 SIT-UPS DIES 3 DAYS LATER

(*Contd.*)

Honour for 'best parents'

Awards given for the child's attendance, tidy appear... education, and discipline

Staff Reporter

...BAD: Awards for 'Best Teacher' and 'Best Student' ... commonplace. Taking it to the next higher level, a government school in ... city has pres... awards 'Best Par...

School ... derecognised

RAJAHMUNDRY: East Godavari District Education Officer Srinivasulu Reddy has recommended that the Collector derecognise a school at ... where a teacher allegedly forced a student to drink his own ... on Wednesday.

బాలుడ్ని చితకబాదిన వార్డెన్‌పై కేసు

Provide toilets in schools in six months, orders court

J. Venkatesan

NEW DELHI: The Supreme Court on Wednesday directed all States and Union Territories that basic toilet fa... ...ticular to girl ... in all

Mid-day meals for pregnant women and children too

...itious food will be provided to mothers who are found to ...

- The pay of anganwadi workers and assistants will be increased

School authorities want traumatised girl to ...

PARWEZ HAFEEZ | DC
KOLKATA, JULY 11

...ically challenged student participates in a painting competition ... Biodiversity in the Place Where I Live, organised by ... association with National Green Corps and Jawaha... ...nd on Monday.

...ols multiplied by 27 per cent ...en 2002-09, says NCERT survey

...ional Council of Educational Research and Training (NCERT) ... suggest that one-fifth of the primary schools did not ... drinking water, three out of ... were without usable ... and about half of ... did not have play...

(*Contd.*)

Schoolgirl raped, set on fire

GIRL STUDENTS MOLESTED BY TEACHER

DC CORRESPONDENT

Student alleges repeated rape

Girl molested, filmed by yout[hs]

DC CORRESPONDENT
HYDERABAD, JULY 15

Students beaten up in Khammam district

Six schoolgirls lodge complaint against teacher

Girl lured, impregnated by teacher

Class X student raped

Boy dies after 'torture' at school

14-year-old Ismail forced to do over 300 sit-ups

Principal held for caning LKG student

(*Contd.*)

Teacher thrashed for 'misbehaving' with girl
Children without uniforms sent away
CORPORAL
CLASS I STUDENT BEATEN FOR MISSING SCHOOL
TUTOR GETS 10-YR JAIL FO RAPING MINOI
Other Stories
MAN SODOMISES, KILLS GRANDSON, GETS 30-YEAR JAIL
School loses recognition
Children sniff to a 'high'
correction fluids, freely available, rampant in
AVOIDABLE TRAGEDY
Teachers in dark over first aid
DC CORRESPONDENT
HYDERABAD, SEPT. 16
MEDICAL EMERGENC
No first aid training at schools
No toilets yet in 6,075 AP schools
DC CORRESPONDENT
HYDERABAD, OCT. 29
Students pour out their anguish before official
conducted into alleged beating of girls at KGBV by a teacher for securing less marks in
room, two schools
staff of State-run schools in Malakpet
nodated in a single room
MONDAY, NOVEMBER 26, 2012
MADRASA STAFF SHOWS PORN TO STUDENTS, HELD
DC CORRESPONDENT
HYDERABAD, JULY 18
acher booked
xy' lesson

Module Awareness on CRC for Teachers

1. Non-Discrimination–Art. 2
2. Survival and Development–Art. 3
3. Views of the Child – Art. 6
4. Participation – Art. 12

Who are children ???

child is precious – handle with care

child is unique, innocent – know it

child is sensitive, is future protected ???

So

Respect the child

Listen to the child

Teach the child

Make the child

What is your role ???

As fellow adult ???

Know the rights of the children

Observe the children around you

Make others also to observe the children

Keep the child happy always

Nurture to biosson and

Allow the child to grow and live

Creat a COMPLETE living

visual your future in children

create a wonderful colourfu world around-

at present and in future

This is MY responsibility

This is YOUR responsibility

This is Everybody's responsibility

Give their RIGHTS make them Responsible

Don't Discriminate, Abuse,

Never put down the child

Glance at the children under different circumstances
See Ground realities !!!!

What is our role as a teacher

1. Know your RESPONSIBILITY
2. Know CHILDRENS RIGHTS
3. PROTECT children's rights

CRC-CHILD RIGHTS CONVENTION

- *In 1959, the UN General Assembly adopted the Declaration of the Rights of the Child*
- *First major international instrument exclusively devated to children's rights.*
- *The Declaration provided the moral and legal basis for developing a binding treaty on the rights of the child.*
- *The UN proclaimed 1979 as the Year of the Child*

CHILD RIGHTS COVENTION

Part 1–Child rights–Art. (1-41)

Part 2–Committee–Art. (42-45)

Part 3–Implementation–Art. (46-54)

Rights of Children

- Survival
- Development
- Protection
- Participation
- Education

- Know that children are special and always do what is best to us.
- Listen to us when we tell you how we are thinking and feeling, when we are upset, when we have problems or worries or when we need to talk to your. We may not be able to use words, so take notice of what we do and how we look because this can tell you what we are thinking and feeling.
- Give us the very best possible care and the comfort we need.
- Let us and our families be who we want to be, whatever our beliefs and customs, so that we feel safe at all times.
- Let our families and others who are important to us be with us, to care for us and love us.
- No matter how big or small we are, tell us what we need to know in a way we can understand.
- Let us have a say in things that are happening to us now and in the future.
- No one has the right to harm us, not doctors or nurses and not even our Mums or Dads. Protect us always from anyone who would harm us or treat us badly.
- Our bodies belong to us. Ask us if you want to share information about us and make sure we stay safe. Give us space and privacy, as well as the chance to be with others grow up to be the best
- Help us grow up to be the best we can.
  Let us learn, let us play and discover some things for ourselves.
- When you care for us, make sure that everyone is working together to do what is best for us until we are grown up and can decide things for ourselves.

Source: UNICEF.

UNICEF Leaflet Containing Summary of UNCRCC

The Government should protect children from work that is dangerous, or might harm their health or their education.

The Government should provide ways of protecting children from dangerous drugs.

The Government should protect children from sexual abuse.

The Government should make sure that children are not abducted or sold.

Children should be protected from any activities that could harm their development.

Children who break the law should not be treated cruelly. They should not be put in prison with adults and should be able to keep in contact with their families.

Governments should not allow children under 16 to join the army.

Children who have been neglected or abused should receive special help to restore their self-respect.

Children who are accused of breaking the law should receive legal help. Prison sentences for children should only be used for the most serious offences.

If the laws of a particular country protect children better than the articles of the Convention, then those laws should stay.

The Government should make the Convention known to parents and children.

Whose responsibility?

Children's rights are a special case because many of the rights laid down in the Convention on the Rights of the Child have to be provided by adults or the state.

However, the Convention also refers to the responsibilities of children, in particular to respect the rights of others, especially their parents (Article 29).

If every child, regardless of their sex, ethnic origin, social status, language, age, nationality or religion has these rights, then they also have a responsibility to respect each other in a humane way.

If children have a right to be protected from conflict, cruelty, exploitation and neglect, then they also have a responsibility not to bully or harm each other.

If children have a right to a clean environment, then they also have a responsibility to do what they can to look after their environment.

If children have a right to be educated, then they have the obligation to learn as much as their capabilities allow and, where possible, share their knowledge and experience with others.

If all children have a right to a full life, then they should also lend help so the needy, the disadvantaged, and the victims of discrimination also enjoy this right.

If children have a right to freedom of thought, conscience and religion, then they also have the obligation to respect other's thoughts or religious principles.

You can probably think of many more.

Derived from a Universal Declaration of Human Responsibilities, by an organisation called World Goodwill, composed of ex-heads of state.

Check out UNICEF UK's website for children and young people: www.therightssite.org.uk

UNICEF website: www.unicef.org.uk

For further free copies of this leaflet call the UNICEF Helpdesk: 0870 606 3377
Quote code: 32124

Cartoons by Buck

This leaflet contains a summary of the United Nations Convention on the Rights of the Child

A convention is an agreement between countries to obey the same law. The United Kingdom of Great Britain and Northern Ireland agreed to obey (ratified) the Convention on the Rights of the Child on 16 December 1991.

That means our government now has to make sure that every child has all the rights in the Convention, except the two they have 'reservations' about (Articles 10 and 37).

Everyone under 18 years of age has all the rights in this Convention.

The Convention applies to everyone, whatever their race, religion, abilities; whatever they think or say, whatever type of family they come from.

All organisations concerned with children should work towards what is best for each child.

Governments should make these rights available to children.

Governments should respect the rights and responsibilities of families to direct and guide their children so that, as they grow, they learn to use their rights properly.

All children have the right to life. Governments should ensure that children survive and develop healthily.

All children have the right to a legally registered name, and nationality. Also the right to know and, as far as possible, to be cared for by their parents.

Governments should respect children's right to a name, a nationality and family ties.

Children should not be separated from their parents unless it is for their own good. For example, if a parent is mistreating or neglecting a child. Children whose parents have separated have the right to stay in contact with both parents, unless this might hurt the child.

Families who live in different countries should be allowed to move between those countries so that parents and children can stay in contact, or get back together as a family.

Governments should take steps to stop children being taken out of their own country illegally.

Children have the right to say what they think should happen, when adults are making decisions that affect them, and to have their opinions taken into account.

Children have the right to get and to share information, as long as the information is not damaging to them or to others.

Children have the right to think and believe what they want, and to practise their religion, as long as they are not stopping other people from enjoying their rights. Parents should guide their children on these matters.

Children have the right to meet together and to join groups and organisations, as long as this does not stop other people from enjoying their rights.

Children have a right to privacy. The law should protect them from attacks against their way of life, their good name, their families and their homes.

Children have the right to reliable information from the mass media. Television, radio, and newspapers should provide information that children can understand, and should not promote materials that could harm children.

Both parents share responsibility for bringing up their children, and should always consider what is best for each child. Governments should help parents by providing services to support them, especially if both parents work.

Governments should ensure that children are properly cared for, and protect them from violence, abuse and neglect by their parents, or anyone else who looks after them.

Children who cannot be looked after by their own family must be looked after properly, by people who respect their religion, culture and language.

When children are adopted the first concern must be what is best for them. The same rules should apply whether the children are adopted in the country where they were born, or if they are taken to live in another country.

Children who come into a country as refugees should have the same rights as children born in that country.

Children who have any kind of disability should have special care and support, so that they can lead full and independent lives.

Children have the right to good quality health care, to clean water, nutritious food, and a clean environment, so that they will stay healthy. Rich countries should help poorer countries achieve this.

Children who are looked after by their local authority, rather than their parents, should have their situation reviewed regularly.

The Government should provide extra money for the children of families in need.

Children have a right to a standard of living that is good enough to meet their physical and mental needs. The Government should help families who cannot afford to provide this.

All children and young people have a right to a primary education, which should be free. Wealthy countries should help poorer countries achieve this. Discipline in schools should respect children's human dignity. Young people should be encouraged to reach the highest level of education they are capable of.

Education should develop each child's personality and talents to the full. It should encourage children to respect their parents, and their own and other cultures.

Children have a right to learn and use the language and customs of their families, whether these are shared by the majority of people in the country or not.

All children have a right to relax and play, and to join in a wide range of activities.

(*Contd.*)

Article 28
Children have a right to an education. Discipline in schools should respect children's human dignity. Primary education should be free. Wealthy countries should help poorer countries achieve this.

Article 29
Education should develop each child's personality and talents to the full. It should encourage children to respect their parents, and their own and other cultures.

Article 30
Children have a right to learn and use the language and customs of their families, whether these are shared by the majority of people in the country or not.

Article 31
All children have a right to relax and play, and to join in a wide range of activities.

Article 32
The Government should protect children from work that is dangerous, or that might harm their health or their education.

Article 33
The Government should provide ways of protecting children from dangerous drugs.

Article 34
The Government should protect children from sexual abuse.

Article 35
The Government should make sure that children are not abducted or sold.

Article 36
Children should be protected from any activities that could harm their development.

Article 37
Children who break the law should not be treated cruelly. They should not be put in prison with adults and should be able to keep in contact with their families.

Article 38
Governments should not allow children under 15 to join the army. Children in war zones should receive special protection.

Article 39
Children who have been neglected or abused should receive special help to restore their self-respect.

Article 40
Children who are accused of breaking the law should receive legal help. Prison sentences for children should only be used for the most serious offences.

Article 41
If the laws of a particular country protect children better than the articles of the Convention, then those laws should stay.

Article 42
The Government should make the Convention known to all parents and children.

The Convention on the rights of the child has 54 articles in all. Articles 43-54 are about how adults and governments should work together to make sure all children get all their rights.

A convention is an agreement between countries to obey the same law. When the government of a country ratifies a convention, that means it agrees to obey the law written down in that convention.

The United Kingdom of Great Britain and Northern Ireland ratified the Convention on the Rights of the Child on 16 December 1991. That means our government now has to make sure that every child has all the rights in the Convention.

Registered Charity No. 1072612

unicef
United Nations Children's Fund

Summary of the UN Convention on the Rights of the Child

Article 1
Everyone under 18 years of age has all the rights in this Convention.

Article 2
The Convention applies to everyone whatever their race, religion, abilities, whatever they think or say, whatever type of family they come from.

Article 3
All organisations concerned with children should work towards what is best for each child.

Article 4
Governments should make these rights available to children.

Article 5
Governments should respect the rights and responsibilities of families to direct and guide their children so that, as they grow, they learn to use their rights properly.

Article 6
All children have the right to life. Governments should ensure that children survive and develop healthily.

Article 7
All children have the right to a legally registered name, and nationality. Also the right to know and, as far as possible, to be cared for, by their parents.

Article 8
Governments should respect children's right to a name, a nationality and family ties.

Article 9
Children should not be separated from their parents unless it is for their own good. For example, if a parent is mistreating or neglecting a child. Children whose parents have separated have the right to stay in contact with both parents, unless this might hurt the child.

Article 10
Families who live in different countries should be allowed to move between those countries so that parents and children can stay in contact, or get back together as a family.

Article 11
Governments should take steps to stop children being taken out of their own country illegally.

Article 12
Children have the right to say what they think should happen, when adults are making decisions that affect them, and to have their opinions taken into account.

Article 13
Children have the right to get and to share information, as long as the information is not damaging to them or to others.

Article 14
Children have the right to think and believe what they want, and to practise their religion, as long as they are not stopping other people from enjoying their rights. Parents should guide their children on these matters.

Article 15
Children have the right to meet together and to join groups and organisations, as long as this does not stop other people from enjoying their rights.

Article 16
Children have a right to privacy. The law should protect them from attacks against their way of life, their good name, their families and their homes.

Article 17
Children have the right to reliable information from the mass media. Television, radio, and newspapers should provide information that children can understand, and should not promote materials that could harm children.

Article 18
Both parents share responsibility for bringing up their children, and should always consider what is best for each child. Governments should help parents by providing services to support them, especially if both parents work.

Article 19
Governments should ensure that children are properly cared for, and protect them from violence, abuse and neglect by their parents, or anyone else who looks after them.

Article 20
Children who cannot be looked after by their own family must be looked after properly, by people who respect their religion, culture and language.

Article 21
When children are adopted the first concern must be what is best for them. The same rules should apply whether the children are adopted in the country where they were born, or if they are taken to live in another country.

Article 22
Children who come into a country as refugees should have the same rights as children born in that country.

Article 23
Children who have any kind of disability should have special care and support, so that they can lead full and independent lives.

Article 24
Children have the right to good quality health care, to clean water, nutritious food, and a clean environment, so that they will stay healthy. Rich countries should help poorer countries achieve this.

Article 25
Children who are looked after by their local authority, rather than by their parents, should have their situation reviewed regularly.

Article 26
The Government should provide extra money for the children of families in need.

Article 27
Children have a right to a standard of living that is good enough to meet their physical and mental needs. The Government should help families who cannot afford to provide this.

Source: UNICEF (see subsequent pages also).

Children Rights and Responsibility

Summary of the UN Convention on the Rights of the Child

- **Article 1**—Everyone under 18 years of age has all the rights in this Convention.
- **Article 2**—The Convention applies to everyone whatever their race, religion, abilities, whatever they think or say, whatever type of family they come from.
- **Article 3**—All organisations concerned with children should work towards what is best for each child.
- **Article 4**—Governments should make these rights available to children.
- **Article 5**—Governments should respect the rights and responsibilities of families to direct and guide their children so that, as they grow, they learn to use their rights properly.
- **Article 6**—All children have the right to life. Governments should ensure that children survive and develop healthily.
- **Article 7**—All children have the right to a legally registered name, and nationality. Also the right to know and, as far as possible, to be cared for, by their parents.
- **Article 8**—Governments should respect children's right to a name, a nationality and family ties.
- **Article 9**—Children should not be separated from their parents unless it is for their own good. For example, if a parent is mistreating or neglecting a child. Children whose parents have separated have the right to stay in contact with both parents, unless this might hurt the child.
- **Article 10**—Families who live in different countries should be allowed to move between those countries so that parents and children can stay in contact, or get back together as a family.
- **Article 11**—Governments should take steps to stop children being taken out of their own country illegally.
- **Article 12**—Children have the right to say what they think should happen, when adults are making decisions that affect them, and to have their opinions taken into account.
- **Article 13**—Children have the right to get and to share information, as long as the information is not damaging to them or to others.
- **Article 14**—Children have the right to think and believe what they want, and to practise their religion, as long as they are not stopping other people from enjoying their rights. Parents should guide their children on these matters.
- **Article 15**—Children have the right to meet together and to join groups and organisations, as long as this does not stop other people from enjoying their rights.
- **Article 16**—Children have a right to privacy. The law should protect them

from attacks against their way of life, their good name, their families and their homes.

- **Article 17**—Children have the right to reliable information from the mass media. Television, radio, and newspapers should provide information that children can understand, and should not promote materials that could harm children.
- **Article 18**—Both parents share responsibility for bringing up their children, and should always consider what is best for each child. [Governments should help parents by providing services to support them, especially if both parents work.
- **Article 19**—Governments should ensure that children are properly cared for, and protect them from violence, abuse and neglect by their parents, or anyone else who looks after them.
- **Article 20**—Children who cannot be looked after by their own family must be looked after properly, by people who respect their religion, culture and language.
- **Article 21**—When children are adopted the first concern must be what is best for them. The same rules should apply whether the children are adopted in the country where they were born, or if they are taken to live in another country.
- **Article 22**—Children who come into a country as refugees should have the same rights as children born, in that country.
- **Article 23**—Children who have any kind of disability should have special care and support, so that they can lead full and independent lives.
- **Article 24**—Children have the right to good quality health care, to clean water, nutritious food, and a clean environment, so that they will stay healthy. Rich countries should help poorer countries achieve this.
- **Article 25**—Children who are looked after by their local authority, rather than by their parents, should have their situation reviewed regularly.
- **Article 26**—The Government should provide extra money for the children of families in need.
- **Article 27**—Children have a right to a standard of living that is good enough to meet their physical and mental needs. The Government should help families who cannot afford to provide this.
- **Article 28**—Children have a right to an education. Discipline in schools should respect children's human dignity. Primary education should be free. Wealthy countries should help poorer countries achieve this.
- **Article 29**—Education should develop each child's personality and talents to the full. It should encourage children to respect their parents, and their own and other cultures.
- **Article 30**—Children have a right to learn and use the language and customs of their families, whether these are shared by the majority of people in the country or not.
- **Article 31**—All children have a right to relax and play, and to join in a

wide range of activities.

- **Article 32**—The Government should protect children from work that is dangerous, or that might harm their health or their education.
- **Article 33**—The Government should provide ways of protecting children from dangerous drugs.
- **Article 34**—The Government should protect children from sexual abuse.
- **Article 35**—The Government should make sure that children are not abducted or sold.
- **Article 36**—Children should be protected from any activities that could harm their development.
- **Article 37**—Children who break the law should not be treated cruelly. They should not be put in prison with adults and should be able to keep in contact with their families.
- **Article 38**—Governments should not allow children under 15 to join the army. Children in war zones should receive special protection.
- **Article 39**—Children who have been neglected or abused should receive special help to restore their self-respect.
- **Article 40**—Children who are accused of breaking the law should receive legal help. Prison sentences for children should only be used for the most serious offences.
- **Article 41**—If the laws of a particular country protect children better than the articles of the Convention, then those laws should stay.
- **Article 42**—The Government should make the Convention! known to all parents and children.

The Convention on the rights of the child has 54 articles in all. Articles 43-54 are about how adults and governments should work together to make sure all children get all their rights.

A convention is an agreement between countries to obey the same law. When the government of a country ratifies a convention, that means it agrees to obey the law written down in that convention.

The United Kingdom of Great Britain and Northern Ireland ratified the Convention on the Rights of the Child on 16 December 1991. That means our government now has to make sure that every child has all the rights in the Convention.

Whose Responsibility

Children rights are a special case because many of the rights laid down in the Convention on the Rights of the Child have to be provided adults or the State.

However, the Convention also refers to the responsibilities of children, in particular to respect the rights of others, specially their parents (Article 29).

Here are some suggestions of the responsibilities that could accompany rights...

If very child, regardless of their sex, ethnic origin, social status, language, age, nationality or religion has these rights, then they also have a responsibility to respect each other in a humane way.

If children have a right to be protected from conflict, cruelty, exploitation and neglect, then they also have a responsibility not to bully or harm each other.

If children have a right to a clean environment, then they also have a responsibility to do what they can to look after their environment.

Index

Abuse, 12–13, 25, 38, 42, 44, 73, 110, 116
    drug, 13
    sexual, 44, 73
Administrative authorities, 15
Adult offenders, 25
Afghan children, 43
Andhra Pradesh State Human Rights Commission, 36
Asian Centre for Human Rights in India, 32
Audio-visual aids, 64
Australian Federal Government and Australian Human Rights Commission, 42
Average School Buildings, 83
Awareness Levels of Teachers on Child Rights, 111
Awareness of teachers, 44–45, 58–59
Awareness raising, 19

Basic child rights, 75
Basic Schools in Ghana, 44
Bear Educational Expenses, 108
Body languages, 72
Bright Child Drop-Out, 107
Building, District-wise Aeration in School, 86
Building provision, 118

Central African Republic (CAR), 42–43
Centre for Child Rights, 23
Child
    abuse, 18, 42, 44, 56
    budget analysis, 23
    care, 26
    centric methods, 29
    death, 44
    development, 23, 27–28
    disabled, 68
    friendly practices, 78–81, 116
    hopeless, 110
    innocent, 110
    interaction, 52–53
    jurisprudence, 39
    labour, 21, 26–27, 37, 39, 56, 101, 108
    marriage, 12, 24, 46, 68
    mortality, 35, 41–42
    panchayats, 120
    poor, 41
    pornography, 18, 24
    poverty, 26
    personality, 44
    rights, 19
    prostitution, 18, 24, 44
Childhood diseases, 21
Child Labour Act, 105
Child Protection Foundation (CPF), 44
Children
    development of, 13
    meritorious, 118
    mischievous, 95
    missing, 32, 44

precious, 13
school drop-out, 53
street, 28, 38, 46
trafficked, 38
tribal, 46
clubs, 120
panchayats, 120
perceptions, 29, 47, 114–15
courts, 31
Child Rights Act, 31
Child rights
awareness training, 44
information network (CRIN), 19
treaties, 18
violation, 36, 120
Child soldiers, 18, 35, 43
Child-teacher interaction, 52–53
Child to Child Interaction, 96
Class
differentiation, 41
imbalances, 40
inequalities, 40
Classroom
cleanliness, 70
environment, 50, 53, 61
experience, 44
observations, 50, 52–53, 95
teaching, 54, 113
Class strength, 69
Commission for Protection of Child Rights Act, 21–22
Compulsory education, 22, 28, 39
Constitution of India, 21, 26, 30–31, 41
Contemporary state policy, 44
Corporal punishment, 29, 37, 40, 45, 58, 80, 95, 112, 115
Cultural dimensions, 117

Dalit student, 33
Day school practices, 60
Death penalty, 25–26
Delhi Commission for Protection of Child Rights (DCPCR), 32, 38
Democratic Republic of the Congo (DRC), 43
Deprivation, 38, 40
Digital classroom, 67
Direction to Protect Children, 27
Directive Principles of State Policy, 30
District-wise
adequate furniture, 90
availability of scavenger, 92
child-friendly schools, 95, 98
disciplinary practices, 97
drinking water, 92
health camps, 93
laboratory, 93
playground, 89
school ambience, 88
separate toilets for girls and boys, 91
teaching learning material, 94
ventilation, 86
Domestic Violence Act, 27
Domestic worker, 42, 105
Dress pattern, 73–74

Early marriage, 34, 36
Economic exploitation, 25, 56
Elementary education, 23
Emotional dimension, 72, 112, 117
Etiquette, 65, 75, 77
European Network of Ombudsmen for Children (ENOC), 19

Facilities
academic, 50
adequate, 60–61, 64
basic, 51
excellent, 82
good, 67–68, 70
inadequate, 116
laboratory, 118
recreation, 53
scavenging, 77
toilet, 53
Female foeticide, 24

Floral arrangements, 108
Forced prostitution, 44
Friendly approaches, 60
Fundamental freedom, 13

Gender
  awareness, 35
  discrimination, 12, 34–35, 117
  equality, 23, 35
  equity, 44
  gap, 43
  injustice, 24
  related abuses, 34
General Assembly, 101
Goa Children's Act, 45
Governmental agencies, 30
Group Report on Child Protection, 23

Hague Convention, 18
Harsh punishment, 104
Hazardous employment, 31
Health
  camps, 53, 63, 76, 93, 118
  care, 18, 38
  checkups, 76
  dimension, 75
  measures, 117
Healthy boundaries, 44
Human rights, 13, 16, 31
Hygiene
  dimensions, 81
  practices, 76, 112

Indian Penal Code, 27, 38
Institution-building processes, 21
Internal Displacement Monitoring Centre (IDMC), 43
Internet and Child Rights, 44
Interpersonal skills, 65

Juvenile justice, 31

Labour
  bonded, 31, 46
  daily wage, 106
  domestic, 107
  family child labour/domestic, 12
Learning material, 34, 52, 61, 94
Life skills, 43
Life stories, 66
Little Tom Primary School, 37
Lord's Resistance Army (LRA), 43
Lower Kindergarten (LKG), 59

Material abandonment, 31
Maternal deaths, 34
Media posters, 118
Mid-day meals, 33, 36, 53, 70, 77–78, 93, 106, 118
Millennium Development Goals (MDGs), 35, 41
Million street children, 38
Monitoring Children's Rights, 18
Mortality rates, High urban, 33

National Advisory Council, 22–23
National Commission for Protection of Child Rights, 38–40
National Convention on Displaced People, 39
National Policy of Children, 26
Navodaya Vidyalaya, 32–33
Negligent attitude of parents, 12
Neonatal health, 34
Newborn health, 34
Nirmal Chhaya Complex, 32
Non-governmental organisations, 18
Nuclear family, 26, 103
Nutrition deficiency, 104
Nutrition dimension, 71
Nutrition of children, 36, 52

Open ended questions, 50–52, 64, 116
Out-of-school children, 41

Parental Relations, 65, 69

Parent-teacher meetings, 110
Participatory
  dialogue, 28
  process, 27
Personal
  attention, 72
  hygiene, 77
  liberty, 31
Physical
  dimensions, 71, 112, 117
  education, 79
  punishment, 72, 117
Poverty, 12, 26, 34, 36, 43, 105, 107–8
Primary health centres, 76
Private schools function, 104
Protection of Child Rights Act, 31
Protection of Rights of Children, 22
Psychological dimensions, 72
Public education, 24

Quality education, 28

Ratification, instrument of, 16–17
Recreation material, 118
Recruitment risk, 42
Remedial class, 113
Remedial instruction, 115
Right of Children, 28
Right to Education Bill, 45
Right to Information Act, 32
RTE Act, 11, 28, 31
Running water in Toilets, 92
Rural education gaps, 35
Rural localities, 85

Safety for Girl Child, 109
Scavengers, 33, 92, 117
School(s)
  aided, 59
  ashram, 46
  building, 53, 62, 82, 84–86
  campus, 74
  co-education, 74
  curriculum, 28
  drop-outs, 28
  environment, 51, 62, 70, 114
  expenses, 108
  fees, 40, 106, 108
  health camps, 117
  libraries, 19
  management committee, 37
  managements, 37, 59, 111–12
  private co-education, 108
  rural, 86, 93
  strength, 68, 104
  urban, 86, 118
Screening tests, 37
Security for Girl Children, 109
Separate Toilets for Girls and Boys, 91
Sexual dimension, 71, 73
Sexual exploitation, 18, 35, 43–45, 56
Sexual harassment, 52
Shelter homes, 32
Skilled health worker, 42
Social acceptance, 111
Social dimensions, 73–74
Social justice, 41
Social rights, 13
Social skills, 41
Social welfare institution, 15
Socio-economic background, 53, 60, 64, 104
State Advisory Council, 23
State Agency for Child Protection, 44
Subject centric curriculum, 28

Teachers
  awareness levels of, 29, 58, 111
  awareness, 58–59
  friendly, 64–65
  interaction, 53
  loving, 68
  male, 49, 59
  qualification, 58, 78–79
  regular, 114
  self projections, 98
  undergraduate, 58

Teaching ability, 44
Teaching aids, 50, 67
Teaching Learning Material (TLM), 53, 62, 93–94, 97, 114, 118
Teaching learning strategies, 50
Trafficking, 13, 37, 39, 43–45
Tribal districts, 36

UKIERI funds research on Children, 43
Under-five deaths, 33, 35
UNICEF, 13–14, 16, 18, 26, 28, 30, 33–36, 44, 100
United Nations Convention, 15, 21, 24, 39, 42
Universality of Child Rights, 39
Urban localities, 90
Urban slums, 105, 108–9

Vaccination, 76
Vedic Maths, 103
Vegetable vendors, 108

Watch list on Children and Armed Conflict, 43
Western family values, 25
Women's rights, 35
World Health Organization, 33
World summit for children, 13

Youth Criminal Justice Act (YCJA), 25

Zero tolerance, 39
ZPHS schools, 74